To Everything
a Season

In gratitude for the community of
St. Paul's Memorial Episcopal Church
Charlottesville, Virginia

TO EVERYTHING A SEASON

A Spirituality of Time

BONNIE THURSTON

A Crossroad Book

THE CROSSROAD PUBLISHING COMPANY

NEW YORK

The Crossroad Publishing Company
370 Lexington Avenue, New York, N.Y. 10017

Printed in the United States of America

Library of Congress Cataloging-in-Publication Data
Thurston, Bonnie Bowman.
To everything a season : a spirituality of time /
Bonnie Thurston.
p.   cm.
Includes bibliographical references.
ISBN 0-8245-1784-9
1. Time—Religious aspects—Christianity.
2. Sabbath.   I. Title..
BT78.T38   1999   99-15979
263—dc20   CIP

Contents

Acknowledgments

As the reader will discover in the Introduction, this book arose from the crucible of my own experience of being overworked and out of time. The ideas were first organized for the Ministers and Mates Retreat of the Christian Church (Disciples of Christ) in Georgia and were amended and substantially expanded for the annual parish retreat of St. Paul's Memorial Episcopal Church, Charlottesville, Virginia. Significant sections of the material have been used in a retreat setting with the Elders of the Bethany Memorial Church, Bethany, West Virginia, and with St. Matthew's Episcopal Church, Wheeling, West Virginia. I am grateful to all these people for their warm reception and careful feedback, and especially to the Rev. David Poist of St. Paul's, who suggested that this material might make a helpful book.

I am fortunate to teach in a setting that encourages reflection and writing. My thanks are due to my colleagues and especially my students and the library staff at Pittsburgh Seminary. Thanks also go to my friends, who constantly encourage my work, and in this project, especially to Jane Rotch, who enthusiastically read the earliest draft of the manuscript.

Lynn Quinn, my editor at Crossroad, was encouraging about the project from the beginning. Her extensive and diligent editing of my text has resulted in a much better final product than the manuscript she first received. I owe her a great deal for her expertise, her sensitivity and her patience. With George Miller's proofreading, my manuscripts always reach the press in more accurate form than if I were left to my own devices. I am grateful for Lynn's and George's, and all the loving correction I receive.

Introduction

"God created time and God created plenty of it."
—Irish proverb

One month to the day before he died in 1997, at a midway point in a breakneck intercontinental schedule that marked his sabbatical year—the time for rest and renewal—Henri Nouwen wrote in his journal: "Cork, Wednesday, August 21: Every time I am in Ireland, I am struck with the different rhythm of life. Because of my jet lag, I decided to 'sleep in' until 9:00 a.m. But when I arrived at the breakfast table at 9:30, I was one of the first! No hurry, no urgencies. As they say in Ireland: 'God created time and He created plenty of it.'"[1]

This little book on time is not about the intersection of science and religion. It does not discuss the features of the remarkable common ground that physicists and theologians have discovered in their respective work on time.[2] As fascinating as such theoretical discussion may be, it is not my bailiwick. I am no Steven Hawking; in fact, I have never studied physics. I hope instead to make this book much more reflective and practical. It is born of my own, personal experience with time—experience which seems to be common to many people living in the so-called "developed world" at the end of the millennium.

Almost everybody I know is harried. My friends and acquaintances are in a hurry, having too much to do and too little time in which to do it. I do not, for the most part, live among the "movers and shakers," the jetsetters. My world is the world of middle America, of the church, of the academy. And yet I find that those of us who inhabit this world, too, have great difficulty in coordinating calendars just to have lunch with friends. Finding an evening when two or three couples can get together for dinner is nearly impossible. We say we would like to get together, and we would, but we don't seem to "have time" and can't seem to "make time." Like the little girl in the Bill Keane cartoon who announced, "My watch stopped. It ran out of time!" we live as if we think we are about to "run out of time." We stay "on the run."

In his wonderful book *Anam Cara*, John O'Donohue tells a revealing story. An African explorer was hurrying through the jungle. For several days the Africans carrying his equipment kept pace with him, but on the third morning, they sat down and would not move. After much discussion, the head carrier told the explorer: "We have moved too quickly to reach here; now we must wait to give our spirits a chance to catch up with us."[3] Most of us need to pause to give our spirits time to catch up with us.

Most of my friends have almost no "down time," and again, I think this is the rule rather than the exception. Their lives are "all booked up" with work (everybody is overworked) and family responsibilities, and recreation that sometimes wears them out instead of re-creating them, "relaxation" that requires even more scheduling: tennis, golf, swimming, sports events, symphony, lecture. Nobody, or almost nobody, seems to have any time, as they say in the southern mountains where I grew up, to "just sit."

Clocks and watches are relatively new inventions. Weight-driven mechanical clocks, which replaced water clocks and sundials, appeared about 1300 A.D., and "watches," or portable timepieces, around 1500 A.D. They are now seemingly ubiquitous. They threaten to become idols. Writer and peace activist Jim Forest has noted that "We live in a culture in which the clock has become not only a tool of social coordination, but of domination. It can be seen as the principal religious symbol of the secular age."[4] He relates an experience of accompanying Thich Nhat Hanh, the Buddhist monk, on a speaking tour. While waiting for the elevator doors to open, Forest noted the monk looking at the electric clock above them. The Buddhist said, "A few hundred years ago it would not have been a clock; it would have been a crucifix."[5] Such a radical substitution should give us pause as well.

In his graceful little book on the monastic hours, *The Music of Silence*, another monk, Brother David Steindl-Rast, O.S.B., provides a neat analysis of our situation with regard to time.

> Saturated with information but often bereft of meaning, we feel caught in a never-ending swirl of duties and demands, things to finish, things to put right. Yet as we dart anxiously from one activity to the next, we sense that there is more to life than our worldly agendas.
>
> Our uneasiness and our frantic scrambling are caused by our distorted sense of time, which seems to be continually running out. Western culture reinforces this conception of time as a limited commodity: We are always meeting *dead*lines; we are always short on time, we are always running out of time.[6]

My interest in this phenomenon of "running out of time," of "not having time," is hardly academic. It lacks the cold dispassion of a scientific observer. It grows out of my own life. One morning in 1994, at the end of an academic year, I set out to run a few simple errands. About halfway to the cleaners, I thought, "I am not going to be able to do this. I am too exhausted. In fact, I'm not sure I'm going to be able to get home." Thank God, I did get home, safely. I took off my shoes (that was all I could manage!), crawled into bed, and slept for three hours. When I woke up, I cancelled all my engagements for the next couple of days, slept, rested, read, walked in the woods, prayed, and took a good look at my calendar.

What I found was appalling. I had literally scheduled myself into near collapse. Because I am a widow with no children, it wasn't others' demands on me that led to this place. I was teaching full time at a college, chairing my department and its Master of Arts in Theology program, writing a book, being deeply engaged with the students, serving as the pastor of a small church and as a spiritual director, traveling to speak and lead retreats, trying to keep contact with my family and friends, as well as tending to a "home life" (cooking, gardening, puttering around home). I enjoyed all these activities; I truly felt "called" to most of them. And yet I had driven myself to the edge of physical and spiritual collapse by means of them.

And then the interesting questions started. Why did I have this need to "fill" all my time? Why did I have the sense that there wasn't enough time? Was I really so much in demand? Why did time (or lack thereof) seem to be "the enemy"? I was sure God didn't want me to be in such a state, and taking the whole matter to prayer led me eventually to begin to reflect, theologically and spiritually, on the nature of time itself. And that is how this small book began, as the story of my transformation from a woman who was feeling enslaved by time to one who knows that there is plenty of time. I found peace in the realization that, like everything else, time is the creation of a generous God Who always provides not only the bare essentials, but usually a feast.

But of course the fact that I now "know" that there is plenty of time—that my watch won't "run out of time"—doesn't mean that I always act accordingly. Where do we learn how to do this? Where do we learn to live in the sane and grace-filled way that God intended and provided for when God gifted each of us with the number of our days?

I am concerned that those of us who might be expected to be more in touch with the spirituality of time—those of us in the clergy, especially those of us teaching in the colleges and universities and seminaries—aren't modeling a very sane lifestyle for our parishioners and students. If I as a seminary professor, for example, always seem overscheduled, tired and anxious from "too much to do," my students may decide that this is what life in Christ is *supposed* to look like. God forbid!

I hope this book will suggest that our lives don't have to be this way. What is doesn't have to be. We are free to reshape our times, to be transformed by God's grace, and to live differently. As a guest at my seminary reminded us recently, "Here isn't everywhere and now isn't always." While I don't entirely agree with the latter statement, to the degree that it says "Things don't have to be the way they are right now"— "This too shall pass"—I respond with a hearty "Amen!"

Let me introduce the spirituality of time as I envision it in this book, then, as follows: Chapter one is a reflection on the mystery of time. It's an attempt to help us think about time in the abstract, to look at it from several different perspectives—to consider some of the problems and challenges the concept of time itself presents, but primarily to discover its meaning as gift. It's a somewhat philosophical perspective, and you will recognize many literary examples amongst the biblical references. Chapter two presents a "history" of time, or to be more exact, an overview of how time has been understood in different cultures and throughout many centuries. Chapter three is more practical, exploring the meaning of some "time participles"—familiar phrases such as "making time," "spending time," and "marking time," for example—and asking us to reflect on our responses to them. Chapter four is a reflection on the way we understand time theologically. Each of these chapters has a "time exercise," something specific to do to help us understand both how we think about and how we use time.

Because my premise is that there *is* "enough" time, I devote the rest of the book to the concept of "Sabbath," the fact that when God ordered creation, God built "rest time" or "time out" into its natural rhythm. Chapter five reintroduces this concept of Sabbath, reminding us of some of the ways the writers of Scripture, and later the church, have suggested that time be structured. Chapter six is more practical again, suggesting some ways that we can "make Sabbath" in the midst of our crowded lives. The conclusion returns to the realm of theology to ask that most important of theological questions: So what? What do we do now, today, with this new way of thinking about time?

Probably nothing here will surprise you. I rather hope not. I would prefer to help you to remember what is—the goodness of all that God has created, and Who has created it. My intention is to suggest that most of us need an "attitude adjustment" with regard to time, and that if we make it, we can come to view time as the extravagant gift it is, and to live accordingly, in the *present* moment—in God's eternal Now.

The Gift of Time

"But when the fullness of time had come, God sent his Son, born of a woman, born under the law, in order to redeem those who were under the law, so that we might receive adoption as children."
—Galatians 4:4-5

The "problem" of time is as top a priority as registrations for time management courses would attest, and as current a cultural diversion as the debate on the relative merits of analog over digital watches in the March, 1998, issue of the USAirways magazine article, "Losing Time."[1] When John Marsh wrote his book *The Fullness of Time* fifty years ago, he suggested that in order to understand the "focal problem" of time, time itself must be viewed from a theological perspective, from the point of view of "questions of ultimate reality," from a Godward direction:

> Time is perhaps the focal ... problem of our age. It may seem simple and harmless enough to study its

nature, but the results can be revolutionary. Einstein has brought about a revolution in our understanding of the universe, and Marx has provoked a series of revolutions in history. To study time is more than to seek a definition for a word; for while time is not itself...the ultimate reality, it cannot be properly discussed unless questions of ultimate reality are asked. [2]

Unless we are philosophers, we don't often reflect in the abstract on the nature of much of anything. I daresay you have not recently asked yourself: "What is Truth?" "What is Beauty?" "What is Time?" With the kinds of lives we live, who has time to ask that kind of question?! We need to "take time" for this kind of reflection. Why? Because time is of crucial importance to a religion that claims to be historical. Christianity views time in terms of salvation history. This is what the title of Marsh's book suggests in its allusion to Galatians. For Christians, history is not a random series of events, but part of the eternal plan of God to reconcile humanity to the Divine Life. The writer of Ephesians, for example, speaks eloquently of this when he writes of God's "plan for the fullness of time, to gather up all things in him, things in heaven and things on earth" (1:10), when he sings of "the plan of the mystery hidden for ages in God who created all things" (3:9), and of God's "eternal purpose" (3:11).

Time, in short, *is the locus of God's activity*. In his *Church Dogmatics* (I, 2, 14), Karl Barth reflects that saying "the Word became flesh" means "the Word became time."³ When God became flesh, God became time; revelation became history; history became sacred time. Time is intimately related to the Incarnation. But what is time, in itself?

In one of his autobiographical reflections, *The Sacred Journey*, Frederick Buechner writes an interesting passage on time as children experience it. Let me quote it in its entirety:

> For a child, time in the sense of something to measure and keep track of, time as the great circus parade of past, present, and future, cause and effect, has scarcely started yet and means little because for a child all time is by and large *now* time and apparently endless. What child, while summer is happening, bothers to think much that summer will end? What child, when snow is on the ground, stops to remember that not long ago the ground was snowless? It is by its content rather than its duration that a child knows time, by its quality rather than its quantity—happy times and sad times. . . . Childhood's time is Adam and Eve's time before they left the garden for good and from that time on divided everything into before and after. It is the time before God told them that the day would come when they would surely die with the result that from that point on they made clocks and calendars for counting their time out like money and never again lived through a day of their lives without being haunted somewhere in the depths of them by the knowledge

that each day brought them closer to the end of their lives.[4]

What I knew then [in my childhood], without knowing that I knew, was that to see the dusk, the fireflies, the green lawn, in their truth and fullness is to see them, as a child does, already clothed with timelessness, already freighted with all the aeons still to come during which they and everything else that ever was will continue eternally to be what has been—a part of the wholeness and truth of eternity itself.[5]

What Buechner points out so clearly is that, for children, time is not something to "measure and keep track of." It is not clock time or chronological time as adults experience it. The proof of this is any car trip with a child: "Are we there yet?" "When will we get there?" "How much longer???" These questions are asked much too frequently for the travel comfort of most adults!

For children, time is "real time," that is, time is full of experiences, events, impressions. Time is present time and it is known by its contents. This is the sort of time that Bruce Malina in his fascinating article "Christ and Time: Swiss or Mediterranean?" calls "experienced time."[6] We instinctively grasp this truth about the nature of time, although we forget it; why else would we tell children on their way to a birthday party: "Have a good time!"? Without knowing that they know it, children are aware that time is radical *present*. They know what Brother David Steindl-Rast asserts: Now is the only place where we really are. "We cannot *be* in the future and we cannot *be* in the past; we can only *be* in the present."[7] For children, time "goes on forever." They have little concept of finitude or of death, as their inability to see danger reveals. Children have little sense of change, little sense that things won't always be as they are now.

Buechner is not the only writer to have alluded to the connection between coming to awareness of chronological time and what biblical theology calls "the Fall." He speaks of time before clocks and calendars and knowledge of finitude. "Clock time" is envisioned as a consequence of the Fall in Philip Booth's poem, "Original Sequence," which suggests that the knowledge gained by Adam and Eve when eating the forbidden fruit was the awareness of chronological time.

> Time was the apple Adam ate.
> Eve bit, gave seconds to his mouth,
> and then they had no minute left
> to lose. Eyes opened in mid-kiss,
> they saw, for once, raw nakedness,
> and hid that sudden consequence
> behind an hour's stripped leaves.[8]

The last line of Booth's lengthy poem is especially startling: [God] "reached, and wound the clock." If this theology is less than perfect, it does seem to be the view that, implicitly, many people live with. Time becomes for them the great enemy and taskmaster.

Let's look at time from another perspective, from the point of view of the Hebrew scriptures. The basic attitude toward time found there is that time is cyclical, rooted in the movement of the heavenly bodies that God created at the beginning.

> And God said, "Let there be lights in the dome of the sky to separate the day from the night; and let them be for signs and for seasons and for days and years, and let them be lights in the dome of the sky to give light upon the earth." And it was so. God made the two great lights—the greater light to rule the day and the lesser light to rule the night—and the stars. God set them in the dome of the sky to give light upon the earth.... And God saw that it was good. And there was evening and there was morning, the fourth day.
>
> Genesis 1:14-19

The writer of the Book of Ecclesiastes has picked up this understanding and allows it to serve as a synonym for repeated human experiences. Some passages in this Wisdom book probably date from the time of King Solomon (the tenth century B.C.) and some may be as "late" as the third century B.C. But the writer, whoever he was, sounds very "timely":

For everything there is a season, and a time for every
  matter under heaven:
a time to be born, and a time to die;
a time to plant, and a time to pluck up what is
  planted;
a time to kill, and a time to heal;
a time to break down, and a time to build up;
a time to weep, and a time to laugh;
a time to mourn, and a time to dance;
a time to throw away stones, and a time to gather
  stones together;
a time to embrace, and a time to refrain from em-
  bracing;
a time to seek, and a time to lose;
a time to keep, and a time to throw away;
a time to tear, and a time to sow;
a time to keep silence, and a time to speak;
a time to love, and a time to hate;
a time for war, and a time for peace.

                              Ecclesiastes 3:1-8

For the writer of Ecclesiastes, time, a seemingly endless progression, is marked by what happens in life at various times, or "seasons." The "times" of human life are
recognized by what *takes place* within them, not by a
"place" in a temporal sequence—although God has
given us a sense of that, too: of past, present, future. The
sage understood that it is God Who disposes time, Who
provides time for the seasons of human life. Although

time itself, as Buechner explains, may be grasped in moments of time-less-ness, in the eternal *now*, there is a sense that the nature of time is cyclical; "that which is, already has been" (Eccl. 3:15)—a sense that humans are engaged in a great spiral of repeated events: being born, dying, planting, harvesting, killing, healing, and so forth.

These perspectives on time introduce us to two basic philosophical understandings of time: that time is essentially a succession of moments, endlessly cyclical, known by its contents, and the view that time is the linear march from past, through present, to future. This "modern" view is a relatively recent entry on the scene of human development, arriving after the human inventions of manipulable numbers, zero, and a numerical calendar.

Coincidentally, these two views of time represent two basic cultural orientations as well. Semitic writers such as Ecclesiastes represent the East, which tends to view time as cyclical; the West understands it as linear. For most Western thinkers, time is an abstract dimension, the frame in which events take place.[9] This notion of time is derived from the awareness of change or of the alternation of sameness and difference. We sing as much in Isaac Watts's hymn, "O God, Our Help in Ages Past":

> Time, like an ever rolling stream,
> Bears all her sons away.
> They fly forgotten as a dream
> Flies at the opening day.

The "ever rolling stream" quality is what characterizes the awareness of time for most of us. How do we first become aware of time? How does it become "present," how does it enter our consciousness? My own awakening occurred in a split second—a dramatic moment of revelation in the midst of an otherwise ordinary life event. I remember it vividly. I was standing in the bathroom of the house we moved into when I was about five, looking out the window, and the thought suddenly came to me, "I am going to die." Now, I didn't think I was going to die right away, but the *fact* of my death was staring me in the face right there in our pink-tiled 1950s bathroom. As Paul Tillich points out in *The Eternal Now*, knowing time will end is a sharp way to realize that there is time. That dramatic first awareness of the passing of time has surely shaped how I have thought about and used time all my life.

Exercise: Awakening to Time

As we have learned more about the development of human personality we have come to understand how formative "first" experiences are, how very much we are shaped by our early experiences. Assuming this to be the case (and finding it so in my own life), then our first experiences of or awarenessses of time have probably had a great effect on how we understand and experience time as adults. This time exercise has two, related parts. It asks you to do some "memory work."

First, think back to your biological family, your family of origin or the circumstances in which you grew up. How was time experienced or discussed in your family? Was yours a leisurely family that was relaxed about time and didn't worry about deadlines or being "on time"? Was yours a "hurried" family, always behind schedule and rushing to catch up? Did you grow up in an institution where time was strictly regulated? Were you subject to the schedule at a boarding school? Was your family prepared and methodical in preparing for holidays or, for example, did you wrap the Christmas presents at 3:30 a.m. Christmas morning?

What about your parents? Were they punctual? habitually late? It is instructive to think back about how time was actually "spent" and experienced in early life. My own mother was almost always late in picking me up from meetings. Probably in reaction to those early experiences, I am fanatical about being "on time." In many instances the unspoken messages we received about time shape our own behavior with regard to it.

The second exercise I would suggest is for you to try to remember when time first became present to your consciousness. Have you had some experience that corresponds to my own "awakening?" Was it dramatic? ordinary? How has it shaped your subsequent attitude toward and use of time?

While in some ways "origin is destiny," and we are shaped by our early experiences, it is also true that we don't have to be what we were. And we certainly don't have to duplicate the patterns of our "first families." Often the first step in changing behavior is becoming aware of it. Our attitude toward time can change. To understand time differently we may have to get in touch with how we first experienced and understood it. These questions were designed to help you do just that.

A History of Time

What has been is what will be,
and what has been done is what will be done;
there is nothing new under the sun.
                                    —Ecclesiastes 1:9

Let's look at time from yet another perspective, that of the word itself. Our English word "time" comes from the Old English *tima*—a composite made of the syllables *ti*, meaning to stretch or extend, and *mon*, man. Its Teutonic root means "to extend." In English, time is literally the stretching or the extension of the human—an understanding of the word that certainly rings true for most of us. Current dictionary definitions evolved from the etymology. Time is "the period during which something exists"; "the point at which something occurs"; "a unit of duration"; "a series of recurring instances"; "finite duration."

With the exception of "recurring instances," these rather abstract formulations of time are distinctively Western, the heritage of our Greek ancestors. Oriental minds thought in more concrete terms; the Greek mind speculated. To some degree, the Greeks understood time as an unending pattern, an endless repetition of the same thing, a constant rhythm, but such a description more closely defines the understanding of such ancient near-Easterners as the Egyptians and the Babylonians. This is the voice we hear in the biblical book of Ecclesiastes:

> A generation goes, and a generation comes,
>   but the earth remains forever.
> The sun rises and the sun goes down,
>   and hurries to the place where it rises.
> The wind blows to the south,
>   and goes around to the north,
> round and round goes the wind,
>   and on its circuits the wind returns.
>
> Ecclesiastes 1:4-6

> That which is, already has been; that which is to be, already is; and God seeks out what has gone by.
>
> Ecclesiastes 3:15

It's hard to believe that the Hebrew scriptures, from which our Christian scriptures flow, do not even have a general word for "time," nor is there any clear categorical past/present/future. When Hebrew scripture wants to refer to a point of time, it is called a "day," which denotes not a twenty-four hour period, but the time when something happened. The Hebrew word *eth (oth)* refers to time as a content. Another Hebrew word, *mo 'edh*, has as its root "appoint" and is used in the sense of natural seasons, like the new moon; or festivals of the year, like Passover; and most interestingly, in describing the tent of meeting—literally, the "tent of appointment" where humans meet God.[1] Yet another word, *'olam*, is used in Hebrew scripture for a temporal period whose boundary at least in one direction is not fixed. That usage is perhaps most clear in Psalm 90:1-2: "Lord, you have been our dwelling place in all generations. Before the mountains were brought forth, or ever you had formed the earth and the world, from everlasting to everlasting [that is, from *'olam* to *'olam*], you are God." We have captured the sense of these two words in modern usage: when we make an appointment, we expect to meet someone and that something particular will happen, yet we sing with fervor this line by Isaac Watts: "From everlasting Thou art God, / To endless years the same."

The Hebrew verb doesn't have any real tenses. I wouldn't be surprised if this is the reason the language students at my seminary think Hebrew is "easier" than Greek. Greek has "too many tenses." Very likely, this reflects the more abstract and seemingly precise way the Greeks thought about time: Time is understood in terms of duration, in terms of a moment *of* time in which something happens. But in Hebrew Scripture, a point of time is referred to as a "day," a limited space of time as "days." You will recall that this is how Buechner says children know time, by its "content rather than its duration," its "quality rather than its quantity." Action in relation to time is described in terms of content, as having been completed or not. So in the Hebrew scripture time expresses whether or not something is finished, accomplished.

We hear this powerful Semitic concept of time in the New Testament, for example, as Paul explains the Incarnation: "But when the fullness of time had come, God sent his son, born of a woman..." (Gal. 4:4), and as Jesus preaches "The time is fulfilled, and the kingdom of God has come near" (Mk. 1:15). The Greek word at the root of "fullness" and "fulfilled" in these two quotations is *pleroma* (noun form), and it means to make come true or to bring about, to bring to completion or to finish. The idea is that time has been "filled up" or "completed" or "perfected." The inspired writers used the concept of time in a pregnant sense ("filled") that emphasized what the time contained, what transpired in time. For them, time is event-full. Time is the medium for God's action.[2]

One more aspect of time in Hebrew scripture is vital to our understanding of its meaning and its relevance: temporality is especially important as one of the main characteristics that differentiates the creature from the Creator. Human beings exist in time. God is eternal. Turning again to Psalm 90, we see this point made in several ways:

Lord, you have been our dwelling place in all
generations.
Before the mountains were brought forth,
or ever you had formed the earth and the world,
from everlasting to everlasting, you are God.
You turn us back to dust and say,
"Turn back, you mortals."
For a thousand years in your sight
are like yesterday when it is past,
or like a watch in the night.

Psalm 90:1-4

This same idea is put even more directly by the prophet
Isaiah.

A voice says "Cry out!"
And I say, "What shall I cry?"
All people are grass, their constancy is like the
flower of the field.
The grass withers, the flower fades,
when the breath of the Lord blows upon it;
surely the people are grass.
The grass withers, the flower fades;
but the word of our God will stand forever.

Isaiah 40:6-8

As we move from ancient Semitic thinking into the
world of the Greeks, from the language and culture of
the Hebrew scriptures to that of the Christian scriptures,
we find "time thinking" that is much more akin to ours in

the modern West. Since the Mediterranean/Semitic world was oriented to the present, the reality of time was "experienced time."[3] Our understanding of time as an abstract concept, then, is drawn from the Greeks. According to Plato, time is the "moving image of eternity," the "everlasting image revolving according to number." Time is a reality that is absolute, flowing apart from the events filling it. This is a very different understanding, indeed, from that of the writers of Hebrew scripture. For Aristotle, time is "the number of motion according to before and after." What I think he is saying is that time is the numerable, that is, the countable or measurable, aspect of motion, the measure of change. Building upon Aristotle, St. Augustine looked rather practically at the data of experience and said that time is the distension of the soul, with both the future and the past stretching out from the present of attention.[4]

There are a great many discussions of time in Greek and subsequent Western philosophy, but I'm not sure that their abstract philosophic constructions get us very far. Three Greek words for time, however, will be useful to us as we construct a practical spirituality of time. First, *aion* is the Greek word used to translate the Hebrew word *'olam* mentioned above. Anglicized as "eon," it generally means an "age," a duration or extent of time, or time "endlessly extended." Then there is *chronos*. It is a comparatively rare word in the New Testament, a general word meaning "space of time," "time elapsed," a period of time. This would be "chronological time" as we calculate it with watch and calendar.

Kairos, on the other hand, is a much richer term theologically. It conveys the idea of a point of time, an appointed time, an occasion or opportunity. A "*kairos* moment" is a point especially favorable for an undertaking, an essential or decisive point, when time is understood as fulfillment. In the New Testament, *kairos* is used for time as quality, as a special "place" or "moment" in the execution of God's plan of salvation: for example, in Matthew 26:18, Jesus literally says, "My *kairos* is near," "My *time* is near." He is telling his disciples, "The moment for the fulfillment of my whole unique purpose in life is upon me."

Of the three Greek terms, the word *aion* has retained its meaning most consistently through the ages. But let's look at the difference between the words *chronos* and *kairos* more closely. *Chronos* is chronological time, time as we usually think of it; it is a duration, something measureable. You can hear the Greek root in the English word. *Kairos*, on the other hand, is a particular point of time. In the Nicomachean Ethics, Aristotle defines *kairos* as "the good in the category of time." Paul Tillich notes that "if a special moment of time is good for the fulfillment of something, this moment is *kairos*." *Kairos* is "an outstanding moment in the temporal process, a moment in which the eternal breaks into the temporal, shaking and transforming it and creating a crisis in the depth of human existence."[5] *Kairos* is a crucial category of time in the New Testament's interpretation of history. The Incarnation happened at a particular moment in salvation history, for example. And Jesus did not choose to act unless the time—*kairos*—was perfect: "My hour is not yet come" (John 2:4b). He also knew when the time had accomplished its purpose: "It is finished" (John 19:30). *Kairos* is a special point of time when the self-revealing of God effects salvation.[6] *Kairos* moments are essential and defining moments.

Our lives, too, are made up of *chronos* and *kairos* moments. The *chronos* times of our lives are the events that happen to us. The *kairos* moments are the defining moments in our lives, the moments of new insight, of deeper understanding—moments when everything changes. *Kairos* times are the times in our lives when we can see the hand of God at work. One of the great acts of discernment in the spiritual life is to know which experiences are which. It's not unusual to recognize the *kairos* moments only with 20/20 hindsight.

Exercise: Time Line

This exercise asks you to identify the *chronos* and *kairos* events in your own life. You will need your date book or calendar to remind you of what has happened over the past year. In fact, this exercise works best if you have last year's or even the last couple of years of books to work with.

Choose a specific time period, say six months. Make a list of the major events in the last six months (or the last full year or the last two or three years). This is your *chronos* list. It's going to be a pretty straightforward accounting of what has happened in your life.

Now go back and circle or highlight in some way the events in which God was especially present—when you either felt the presence of God, or in retrospect, you now believe that God was working, leading you, maturing you, molding you. Mark the defining events of the period. This is your *kairos* list.

Note that the *kairos* moments or times are not always experienced as positive. Sometimes they are perceived at the time as being quite negative. Job did not enjoy his sufferings, but they led him to a new understanding of God. Mary Magdalene wept in the garden, thinking her Lord's body had been taken, only to discover the Lord Jesus, Himself, there. *Kairos* moments for the early Christians occurred when they were locked in small rooms and filled with fear. The defining element of *kairos* moments is not how we feel about them, then or now, but our understanding that God is active even—or especially—in these times.

This exercise may take you several days of "mulling over." After you have established your list, you might ask yourself the following questions: Is there any pattern to my *kairos* moments? Are they likely to occur in similar circumstances or to be generated by particular kinds of events? Do they happen as the result of what I plan or do, or are they seemingly "random"? Try to discern whether there are any specific relationships between the *chronos* and *kairos* moments of your life. Does there seem to be some particular "place" or goal toward which God has been leading you by way of your *kairos* moments?

In his journal *Learning to Love*, Thomas Merton reflects on time in a way that illuminates the discussion about *chronos* and *kairos*. Merton notes that the "value" of time "is not in time but in clarity of thought: the moments when we see through time and everything else, and see our way 'through' everything. Time is valuable only for the moments that cut across and through it vertically."[7] What Merton is describing here are these *kairos* moments, moments *in* time when we are able to see *through* time, moments when God's timelessness (the "vertical") is apparent in human time (the "horizontal," or chronological and sequential). I am convinced that *kairos* moments—"peak moments," as described by Abraham Maslow—are much more common than we have been led to believe and are much more available to us than we might have imagined. When we slow down, when we become attentive to the present, when we are rooted in today, in the here-and-now, we permit God to "break through," into our awareness. *Kairos* moments present themselves to us, pure gifts from God.

THREE

Time Participles

Time is an empty form only for abstract, objective reflection, a form that can receive any kind of content; but to him who is conscious of an ongoing creative life it is laden with tensions, with possibilities and impossibilities, it is qualitative and full of significance.[1]

—Paul Tillich

This observation from Paul Tillich's famous book *The Protestant Era* provides an economic summary of the ideas introduced in the previous chapter. In the Hebrew Bible, time is known not as an abstract entity, but as a matrix in which events happen, in which God acts. The New Testament writers understood themselves to be in a time of *kairos*, a propitious moment for the accomplishment of God's plans. For biblical people, then, time is "qualitative and full of significance." How we receive time, how we use the time given to us as gift, how we "fill" our time, is tremendously important.

In the pages to come, you will find some theological

and spiritual reflections on the practical dimension of time, some analysis of how we, in fact, "spend" our time. As disconcerting as the thought may be, I would like you to view time as a commodity, something we expend or use up. Although the metaphor comes to us from commerce, it expresses our existential reality. Each human being is finite. Each of us has only a limited amount of human, chronological time. As much as Madison Avenue would like to help us mask the fact, we are all aging, and eventually, we are all going to die. We Christians rejoice in the sure knowledge that at the end of our individual, human time, our death will mean entry into God, into an eternal Now, with Christ, whom John saw as the "Alpha and the Omega" (Rev. 1:8, 21:6). We rejoice in that fact.

It is a sobering thought, the responsibility to use what time we have well. Many of the parables of Jesus make it clear that we will have to "give an accounting" of how we have used our time. Chapter 25 of Matthew's gospel, for example, presents us with three parables in which judgment depends upon how time is "spent": the parables of the ten bridesmaids, of the talents, and of the sheep and goats. But we must also be alert to whether or not we are being enslaved by time. Do we, in Andrew Marvell's phrase, always feel "time's winged chariot" at our back? Is there a constant sense of too much to do and too little time to do it? Is this anxiety, itself, draining our energy and drawing off the joy of life? And if so, what does it tell us about our life in God?

Notice how we use the word "time" in our daily conversation. As I began to do this myself, I noticed that many common uses of "time" occur in a participial construction, with the word "time" as the object of a participle. Participles, you will remember from high school English class, are verbal forms usually ending in "ing" that can be used as adjectives or nouns. In the sentence "Spending time with you is pleasant," the subject of the sentence is the participle "spending time." What interests me, beyond the grammar, is the number of "time participles" we all use: "keeping time," "spending time," "making time," "taking time," "marking time," "wasting time," and (last but not least!) "killing time" come to mind. What are the associations or connotations carried by these various time participles?

"Keeping time" is a good place to begin our consideration. We might say that someone is "keeping time" to the music if she is tapping her foot "in time," by which we mean that she is beating out the time signature in a musical composition. We frequently hear the phrase as well in the context of a sports event. Someone is "keeping time," that is, measuring the time left in the quarter or the half. A "timekeeper" is one who measures time and tells us how many hours/minutes/seconds/milliseconds have elapsed. These uses of the word come from its archaic association: "keeps" were fortresses or castles where people and livestock and munitions were stored for safety. How can one possibly "keep time"? Time is not a "thing" to be put into jars or pressed between the pages of a book or locked up at the bank in safety deposit boxes. How could one ever really maintain, save, or reserve time? In actuality, "keeping time" is an impossibility.

"Spending time" is an extremely rich concept. We say, "I'd like to spend some time with you," and think very little of it, but it may well be the highest compliment we can pay and the most expensive gift we can give. If time is a commodity of sorts, we do, in fact, "spend" it. If you really want to know someone, examine his or her checkbooks and calendars and datebooks; observe how they spend "their" money and "their" time. How we spend our time and spend our money reveals our priorities and values—they tell us (and others) who we really are. If time, like money, is a commodity, then we need to be attentive to how we spend it.

"Making time" as a turn of phrase probably resonates with busy people. It's actually something of a misnomer. Human beings can't *make* time! We exist in time; we have an "allotted time," but we don't "make time." *God* makes time! Another one of Bill Keane's "Family Circus" cartoons suggests as much as the older sister says to the younger brother, "God invented time to keep everything from happening all at once." Time is one of God's many creations—a gift we, God's creatures, accept, not an item we manufacture. Still, the idea behind "making time" is that of making "space" or carving out time to do something, either something we want to do or something we are obliged or obligated to do. "Making time" usually implies "finding the time" to do something. What is it that you would like to make time to do? And why aren't you doing it?

"Taking time," when we consider it, is also a rather odd expression. To "take" implies to steal or grab something that doesn't belong to us. But this isn't true about time. "When God made time, God made plenty of it." Our times are in God's hands; God gives us the time we need to accomplish what is God's will for us. One cannot "take" or "steal" what is already freely given. "Take time" is somehow a sad but apt metaphor for our acquisitive and grasping culture, isn't it? How interesting that such a positive idea is couched in such negative language! We think of "taking time" as a good thing. We "take time" for people and activities we love. We "take time" for a nap, though to say we "take" a nap is absurd. (Naps take us or they don't happen!) Taking time implies slowing down, being intentional, paying attention. Have you ever "taken time" to reflect on how God would have you "spend" "your" time?

"Marking time" carries another connotation altogether. It suggests that time is moving slowly, and that nothing much is happening. To "mark" something is to set its bounds, to establish its limits. Although to "mark time" originally meant to keep the time of a marching step by standing in place and continuing to move the feet, it has come to mean a static state of readiness. "Marking time" is rather akin to "cooling one's heels"—standing still, waiting, trying to figure out what to do while waiting for something else to happen. Underlying the phrase is a sense that the present moment is somehow lacking, somehow incomplete or wanting. What is *coming* is to be preferred to *what is*. This attitude invites constant stress and disappointment if, indeed, the present moment is the only one we ever have. Somehow, present time must become for us the fullness of time.

"Marking time" has a close relative: "killing time." This vivid expression suggests that the present moment is deficient and must somehow be endured in order to arrive at some better state. But if time is as short and limited as most of us live as if it is, then do we really have any time to kill?

"Wasting time" is universally scorned in our culture. To say "time's a-wasting!" is a warning and a challenge. In business, time wasted is money lost. If we are ruled by our calendars, daytimers and datebooks in our everyday world, wasting time is likely to throw our whole schedule off, to send our day spinning into disarray. What about an opportunity for the Holy Spirit to suggest something new—or even simply to have a moment to reassure us of God's abiding presence and love. We might all be better off if we "wasted" a little time attentively now and again.

I am sure that there are other "time participles" that I've neglected, but I have no doubt that you are already thinking about time in a more practical way. The question now is: How *do* you really "spend" your time?

Exercise: Time Log

At the end of Thomas Merton's journals for 1966-67, published as *Learning to Love*, there is a section entitled "Some Personal Notes, January 1966-March 1966." In a fragmentary sequence Merton writes, "Is time-consciousness the product of our self-awareness *at work?* ... Our time sense is related to our *work* and where we are in it."[2] I think Merton is correct. To bring this somewhat abstract idea a little closer to home, I would suggest that our time sense is related to how we actually fill our time, to what we actually do. Discovering what you actually do with your daily bread—the 24 hours given as gift each day to every human being—is the point of this exercise.

1. Take your datebook or calendar or planner and spend at least 15 to 20 minutes examining where your time goes. Choose an "ordinary" or "representative" week—not vacation, not Holy Week, not Christmas holidays—and make a list of every single thing you did in that week, expanding and filling in, in great detail, the spaces between notes recording appointments and meetings. If you are a student, include time spent in classrooms and labs, studying, researching, working, dating,

walking in the woods, relaxing with friends. If you stay at home with your children, your list might include shopping, driving the children to soccer practice, attending PTA meetings, maintaining your home, overseeing children's activities and the plumber's work, cooking, doing the laundry, having a special lunch with a friend. If you work outside the home, your list might be made up of travel to and from work, how your hours at work are actually invested, hours spent in recreation or volunteering, hours spent at church and working out at the gym. If you are a member of the clergy, your list might begin with pastoral calls, meetings, study, teaching, conducting worship, and build from there.

Don't forget necessary entries that won't be on the calendar: sleeping, running errands, gardening, watching a baseball game, comforting a friend, waiting for hours in a doctor's office or at the motor vehicle department, journaling. A great deal of time is devoted to these myriad activities, which you may not think are important. The idea here is to make as complete and honest a list as you can.

2. After you've made your list and "checked it twice," draw a pie chart or indicate in some way that's meaningful to you the approximate percentages of time you spend in each of the various activities, or divide them into groups of activities, so that you can grasp your week visually. Discover for yourself what the top three time-fillers in your week are. You might be very surprised at

the results. It's best not to judge your list right away—just take a a serious and honest look at what is "filling" your time, just as you might take note of what objects you have in the pantry before you go to the food store.

3. Now that you know exactly what you're working with, you will want to start asking yourself some questions. Is this the way I *want* to spend these precious minutes? If not, how much control do I have to change the way my week works out? It may be that many of the things you can't change can be experienced more positively if you adjust the way you look at all you do—to honor all the ways, large and small, in which you invest yourself as opposed to fighting them all, wrestling with your schedule or being frustrated by the interruptions of life. Look at your list again. What did you "take time" for? Why was it important to do that? What should you have taken time for? What would you have liked to "make time" for? Why didn't you? What do you consider wasted time? Why? What uses of your time brought you joy? What items on your list drained you of energy?

Writing out your reflections is especially helpful. *Take time* to reflect on your answers. Spend some time contemplating those things you want to "make time" for, the things that delight you. You might be surprised to discover that they are not only the things that sustain you and energize you and bring you joy—they are, in fact, the very things that God uses to call you along your unique path; your heart's desires are at the heart of God's call to you. Be willing to "make time" for your heart's desire!

I choose that word deliberately, in the hope of redeeming it from its usual connotation. As a word, "desire" has so often been associated with eroticism that we forget it's a word that simply describes the feeling of yearning or longing. What we desire, what we wish or long for or want, is a pretty good indication of who we are. In *Befriending Our Desires,* a very interesting book on the spiritual life, Philip Sheldrake writes, "Desires are best understood as our most honest experiences of ourselves, in all our complexity and depth, as we relate to people and things around us."[3] Since they speak to us of what we do not have, our desires reveal in us a condition of openness to possibility and to the future.[4] Desire is a great impetus toward the future, toward change and creative action. Our desires can put us deeply in touch with who we really are and who God is calling us to be, what God is calling us toward.

So let's return to the things we make time for but put them in the wider context of our identity and of God's call to us. The interesting question is why we don't do the things we'd like to make time for. You might like to read chapter 55 of the Book of Isaiah, especially the second verse: "Why do you spend your money for that which is not bread, / and your labor for that which does not satisfy?" Are you laboring for something that doesn't satisfy your deepest desires? Ask yourself why you are spending your time on things that you don't desire or that don't delight you. This question may lead you along some interesting paths, especially if you tend to think of "spending time" as being in tension with your duties and responsibilities.

The Christian tradition gives more than one example of attentiveness to these issues. For example, in the tradition of the desert fathers and mothers, young monks and nuns would go out to the desert to ask questions of experienced older monastics, the fathers and mothers of the faith. In response to one such question, Abba Poemen said, "Do not give your heart to that which does not satisfy your heart."[5] At another time, when an elder was asked, "What good thing shall I do, and have life thereby?" the questioner was told: "Whatever you see your soul to desire according to God, do that thing, and you shall keep your heart safe."[6]

What we wish to spend our time on, what we desire to take time for, is not only defining *of* us, but is very likely God's call *to* us. This small quotation from Thomas Merton, which I clipped out of a missions newsletter long ago, focuses the issue powerfully: "If you want to identify me, ask me not where I live, or what I like to eat, or how I comb my hair, but ask me what I am living for, in detail, and ask me what I think is keeping me from living fully for the thing I want to live for." What do you live for? What do you want to live for? If the answers to these two questions are not the same, ask yourself: Why aren't they, and what can I do to harmonize my life?

A Theology of Time

God said to Moses, "I AM WHO I AM." . . .
This is my name forever,
And this my title for all generations."
—Exodus 3:14-15

Let us shift our focus from practical matters to theology. I want to introduce four theological reflections on time. Don't be put off by the word "theology." If you have read this far, you will understand (and I hope appreciate) the material in this chapter.

The first theological reflection has to do with gift. Time is a creation of God, right after the second creation of God—light, which marks time. In the very first chapter of Genesis, God separates light and darkness, calls one day and one night, and there was evening and morning—the beginning of time, which is declared good (see Genesis 1:1-5). Time is one of creation's "goods." As Thomas Merton explains: "Time for the Christian is then the sphere of his spontaneity, a sacramental gift in which he can allow his freedom to deploy itself in joy."[1] But do we receive time as a good gift of God, the matrix in which we can allow "freedom to deploy itself in joy"? Do we experience time as one of the many aspects of creation that we are to enjoy and to steward, or do we experience time as a taskmaster? Do we manage time, or does time manage us? Who ultimately is in control of time?

The Psalmist works it out quite simply. "But I trust in you, O Lord; I say, 'You are my God.' My times are in your hand…" (Ps. 31:14-15a). "My times are in your hand." The understanding of the Psalmist is that it's God Who's in control of time. What would it mean to us really to believe that our times are in God's hand? Mightn't it take us off the hook a bit? Wouldn't it ease a great many of our anxieties? Remember that simple Irish proverb which has revolutionized how I think of time since I first heard it several years ago: "When God made time, God made plenty of it." From God's point of view, there is lots of time, an eternity of it. It follows that there will be plenty of time for what God intends to accomplish. Personally, I have come to believe that God will give me the time to accomplish what it is God's will for me to accomplish, and that is time "enough" for me. That realization has transformed how I think about time, and thus it is changing how I live.

The second theological reflection is that the Bible pushes us to understand time as the matrix of the sacred. The God of Israel, the God of our Lord Jesus Christ, was not a God of place. Unlike the deities of other Ancient Near Eastern peoples, gods associated with temples, sacred springs, or groves of trees, the God of Israel was the God of events, of happenings in time. The fact that the Divinity is manifested in history means that time is holy. "The higher goal of spiritual living is not to amass a wealth of information, but to face sacred moments," Abraham Heschel writes. "Spiritual life begins to decay when we fail to sense the grandeur of what is eternal in time."[2] "The grandeur of the eternal in time"—how many of us can honestly say we are in touch with that aspect of time? If God is not found here, in the *now,* "among the pots and pans," as St. Teresa of Avila would say, God won't be found "then" or "out there" somewhere either.

Living spiritually demands that we be "present tense" people—a distinctly countercultural idea. The enormity of the concept of "God now" bears serious reflection for people who think their relationship with God is important. Like Heschel, Paul Tillich believes: "There is no other way of judging time than to see it in the light of the eternal."[3] What is important about time, in short, is its "God content." In contrast to my friend's comment that "now isn't always," these thinkers are convinced that now, potentially, *is* always, and I would have to agree with them.

The third aspect of time I want to discuss is that time is experienced differently in different situations. In his study *The Direction of Time*, Hans Reichenbach writes: "We know that subjective judgment about the speed of time flow is deceptive; that on some occasions, time seems to pass quickly, on others, it seems to drag, depending, for instance, on whether we are fascinated or bored."[4] Two well-known literary examples illustrate the point quite dramatically.

The first is this familiar passage from Shakespeare's *Macbeth:*

> Tomorrow, and tomorrow, and tomorrow,
> Creeps in this petty pace from day to day,
> To the last syllable of recorded time;
> And all our yesterdays have lighted fools
> The way to dusty death. Out, out, brief candle!
> Life's but a walking shadow, a poor player
> That struts and frets his hour upon the stage,
> And then is heard no more; it is a tale
> Told by an idiot, full of sound and fury,
> Signifying nothing.[5]
>
> *Macbeth,* V.5.18ff

Macbeth articulates an understanding that time creeps by in a slow, pointless shuffle toward the grave. Time moves very slowly, indeed, and toward no very cheerful end. On the other hand, Andrew Marvell's poem, "To His Coy Mistress," presents a different situation and a very different perception of time:

Had we but World enough, and Time,
This coyness, Lady, were no crime.
We would sit down, and think which way
To walk, and pass our long Loves Day.

…

… I would
Love you ten years before the Flood:
And you should if you please refuse
Till the Conversion of the *Jews*.
My vegetable Love should grow
Vaster than Empires, and more slow.
An hundred years should go to praise
Thine Eyes, and on thy Forehead Gaze.
Two hundred to adore each Breast:
But thirty thousand to the rest.
An Age at least to every part,
And the last Age should show your Heart.
For Lady you deserve this State;
Nor would I love at lower rate.

But at my back I alwaies hear
Times winged Chariot hurrying near:
And yonder all before us lye
Desarts of vast Eternity.

…

The Grave's a fine and private place,
But none I think do there embrace.

…

Now let us sport while we may… [6]

Marvell perceives that time is slipping by very quickly, indeed. He'd like to have forever to praise the woman he wants to make love to, but he doesn't have forever. Time is "a'wastin'" and so he says, in effect, we don't have time to wait—let's make love now!

As these two very different examples illustrate, the situation we are in greatly affects our perception of the passing of time. Time spent with a lover flies by and is quickly over. Time spent at a deathbed drags almost unbearably for the loved ones gathered around it. Three hours in the hospital waiting room during critical surgery is in "real time" much longer than three hours spent in one's favorite pastime. According to John O'Donohue, "The quality of our experience always determines the actual rhythm of time. When you are in pain, every moment slows down until it resembles a week. When you are happy and really enjoying your life, time flies."[7] There's time and then there's time.

The final theological aspect of time to ponder here is the fact that the only time we really have is the present moment, now. A little sign in the teller's window at my bank said it well: "*Now* is a gift of God; that is why it is called the *present*." The old cliché is true: the past is gone; the future is yet to be. These facts have profound spiritual implications. One of my students gave me the following poem.[8] Although I know only the author's name and not the source of the poem, I want to include her deep insight into the point we are considering:

I was regretting the past and fearing the future.
Suddenly, my Lord was speaking: "My name is
  'I AM.'"
He paused. I waited. He continued.
"When you live in the past with its mistakes and
    regrets, it is hard.
I am not there. My name is not I WAS.
When you live in the future with its problems and
    fears, it is hard.
  I am not there. My name is not I WILL BE.
When you live in this moment, it is not hard.
  I am here. My name is I AM."

Helen Mallicoat

The "I AM" self-designation of God (see Exodus 3) sets before us the notion of the "radical present" with its truth of God's Presence. If we don't find God in this present moment, we are unlikely to encounter the Divine at all. St. Paul deeply understood this truth and wrote to the Corinthians, "See, now is the acceptable time; see, now is the day of salvation!" (2 Cor. 6:2).

Similarly, St. Paul had just asserted that in Christ there is a new creation (2 Cor. 5:17-21). He quoted Isaiah 49:8, "At an acceptable time I listened to you, / and on a day of salvation I have helped you," and then he asserts that "the acceptable time" is now, the present moment. Another Paul, Paul Tillich, remarked, "Every moment of time reaches into the eternal."[9]

The present, then, is an entré into God's eternity.

Many religions cultivate "attentiveness," or centeredness in the present moment, by means of a variety of prayer disciplines. These are helpful practices for those of us who aren't usually in the present, we who are worrying about the past or anxious about the future, projecting backward and forward and missing the great gift of now. This attentiveness to the present is a wise spiritual discipline, especially for those of us called to pastoral work, where we need to be "present" to people. How can we really listen if we aren't really present?

Recall, if you will, the quotation from Buechner in chapter one that children live in this radical present, that for them moments are "already clothed with timelessness." Evelyn Underhill has written that most of us spend our lives conjugating three verbs: to Want, to Have, and to Do, but the fundamental verb is to Be.[10] Perhaps what we adults must do is to learn simply to be, that is, to shift our time focus from past (was) or future (will be) to present (be). One indication of whether or not we are living primarily in the present is how easily we can answer the question "What am I?" This is not to answer the question "What do I do?" Learning to *be*, apart from all our accomplishments—accepting our status as a human being, not as a human doing—puts us in the presence of the God who discloses the divine identity as "I Am." Being itself may well be the seed of eternity which God plants in the human soul.

Interestingly, the accounts we have of mystical experiences generally in some way attempt to communicate simple "Being," a timeless quality. In his short and very interesting book, *Religions, Values, and Peak-Experiences*, Abraham H. Maslow argues that what we would call "mystical experiences" are much more common than people think. Maslow outlines the nature of these experiences, of which two characteristics are especially germane to our subject:

> In the peak-experience there is a very characteristic disorientation in time and space, or the lack of consciousness of time and space. Phrased positively, this is like experiencing universality and eternity. ... The person in the peak-experiences may feel a day passing as if it were minutes or also a minute so intensely lived that it might feel like a day or a year or an eternity even.[11]

> What has been called the "unitive consciousness" is often given in peak-experiences, i.e., a sense of the sacred glimpsed *in* and *through* the particular instance of the momentary, the secular, the worldly.[12]

It is not only possible but likely that, as Maslow says, we can experience the Eternal in time. What is required of us, I think, is attentiveness, the spiritual equivalent of listening. When, living in the present in profound attentiveness, we experience these "timeless moments" of radical present and Presence, we have come very near, indeed, to God.

I hope this chapter has made clear that time is more than chronology. Time is opportunity. The Hebrew prophets thought of history as a continuum of times, each filled with its content by God, and, therefore, each demanding a response from people. The writers of the New Testament clearly thought of themselves as writing in *the* time of history.[13] And so we Christians have a particular reason to understand that time is a function of divine disclosure. It is the arena of salvation. It is "the means by which God makes use in order to reveal his gracious working."[14] Time is valuable because God has entered time and brought eternity into it. "The time God has for us is constituted by His becoming present to us in Jesus Christ, i.e., *Deus praesens*." Revelation has become history.[15] If, as Christians believe, God has entered time in Jesus Christ, then the value of time has been established. And if the time is fulfilled in Jesus Christ (Gal. 4:4, Eph. 1:10), then time can no longer be regarded as an empty or endless sequence of moments. The coming of the "final fulfillment" has been announced, and has, in fact, begun in the Christ event. And so we, in the words of the writer of Ephesians, must "make the most of the time" (5:16). What that will mean for each one of us is at the heart of the mystery of our individual and God-given vocation.

Exercise: Celebrate Your Seasons

This time exercise may be the most difficult because it asks us to remember something we raised at the outset, something most of us would like to forget: each of us has a finite amount of time available to us, which is to say, we are born and we die. Human life in the flesh has a beginning and an ending. Human life is mortal, finite.

Hans Reichenbach suggests that some of our difficulty with time—our fear of time, if that is a fair way of putting it—is linked to our fear of death. He notes that

> . . .our emotional response to the flow of time is largely determined by the irresistibility of its passing away. The flow of time is not under our control. We cannot stop it; we cannot turn it back; we have the feeling of being carried away by it, helplessly, like a piece of lumber in the current of a river.[16]

Whether we admit it to ourselves or not, somewhere deep within us we know that the inexorable march of time is a death march. "The coming of death is the inescapable result of the irreversible flow of time."[17]

Actually, the biblical writers, especially the writers of the Wisdom literature, approach this matter-of-factly. "For everything there is a season," says the writer of Ecclesiastes, "and a time for every matter under heaven: a time to be born, and a time to die" (3:1-2); God has made "everything suitable for its time" (3:11); God "has appointed a time for every matter, and for every work" (3:17). In Deuteronomy, Moses chides the whole assembly of Israel, "You forgot the God who gave you birth" (32:18). "Precious in the sight of the Lord is the death of his faithful ones," declares the Psalmist (116:15). "Naked I came from my mother's womb, and naked shall I return there; the Lord gave, and the Lord has taken away; blessed be the name of the Lord," says Job (1:21). The biblical witness is universally clear that God is involved in the beginnings and at the ends of the lives of God's beloved people.

God disposes our beginnings and endings. This is how it has always been and how it will always be, except with this twist for Christians: As Thomas Merton noted, human time is now "enclosed between the two advents of Christ."[18] In the words of Paul Tillich, every *kairos* is "implicitly the universal *kairos* and an actualization of the unique *kairos*, the appearance of the Christ."[19] The times of our beginnings and endings are now sanctified by Jesus' coming in humility and His promised return in majesty. And, when that happens, of course, "time will be no more." It is for this reason that the apostle Paul can cry out, "Where, O death, is your victory? Where, O death, is your sting?" (1 Cor. 15:55). The coming and promised return of Jesus Christ have changed how we view birth and death. We are birthed into great possibilities, and we die into greater life. (Note: I am referring here to spiritual realities and not to the theological position known as "dispensationalism.")

This is true of our lives overall. It is most obviously true of our physical life, but it is also true of the movement of our lives. I forget how frequently every cell in the body is replaced, but I do recall that when I learned about it, its speed astonished me. The point is that at any given moment, some things are coming to birth in us, and some things are dying in us. Part of our discernment about our time is to be alert to this process. What is coming to birth in us as individuals? What in us is dying? Or (a slightly different question) what are we dying *to*? These are important questions to examine if we are to have a clear sense of the most fruitful way to "spend our time."

So take some time now to answer those two questions: (1) "What is coming to birth in me?" and (2) "What is dying in me?" Perhaps you can use the lists you've already made to give you some clues. Perhaps those things that you don't want to do, that you feel are a waste of your time, are part of what is dying in you or what you are dying to or what you should be dying to. That some things are dying may be a very good thing. It may be very liberating to discover, if you are middle-aged, for example, that the need for "success" in worldly terms is dying in you. The opposite could also be true: you may have to be coming to terms with the reality that some dreams will

never be realized. If you are settled in a career, you may
have "died" to questions of vocation—either fully blos-
soming in your chosen field or having lost touch with
why you're doing what you do each day. If you have been
a full-time home- and child-caretaker and your children
have left home, you may have to mourn the loss of your
identity and your role—life as you knew it—to make way
for a whole new you, as radical a process as retiring from
work outside the home would be.

It will be helpful to articulate what is dying in you,
and then to discover where you are in the stages of
mourning and acceptance. Perhaps what you desire or
want to make time for is what is meant to be coming to
birth. Perhaps in middle age a new and secure sense of
self is coming to birth in you. Perhaps as a happily mar-
ried woman a new sense of your sexual attractiveness is
coming to birth. But what happens if you are forcing
yourself to make time for what is, in fact, dying in you?
Could this be why you are so exhausted and drained,
why you feel so constantly harried?

So ponder what is coming to birth in you as well as
what is dying. This is a sobering and perhaps even fright-
ening exercise, so do it in the very safe context of the
prayer of the Psalmist: "My times are in your hand"
(31:15a). Whatever is being born in you and whatever is
dying in you is happening under the wonderfully protec-
tive wings of the living God. It might be comforting to do
this exercise after praying Psalm 139, which assures us

that God knows us thoroughly and watches over us wherever we are. "Oh Lord, you have searched me and known me" (v.1). "You hem me in, behind and before, and lay your hand upon me" (v. 5). "In your book were written all the days that were formed for me" (v. 16). Whatever is coming to birth in us, whatever is dying, is doing so in God and in God's loving and benevolent will for us. Our times are in God's hands, and so we are safe.

The Rhythms of Time

*And on the seventh day God finished the work
that he had done, and he rested on the seventh day
from all the work that he had done. So God
blessed the seventh day and hallowed it, because
on it God rested from all the work that he had
done in creation.*

—Genesis 2:2-3

From the moment of creation, time was born in the
rhythms of nature: night followed day; earth had her seasons, and tides their ebb and flow; the moon had cycles,
and the planet humans inhabited had a predictable orbit
around the sun.

How and why humans developed such an artificial
system for keeping track of time can be traced. The span
of a "day" as we know it is divided into 24 hours, but
those hours are divided into 60 minutes, each containing
60 seconds! As Robert Cooke wonders in *Newsday,*
"Why not a day broken down somehow into 10 units, or

20, or 60?" His interview with historian and astronomer Owen Gingerich provides some historical background: "Most of our time units come from the ancient Babylonian sexagesimal system. Thus we have 60 minutes in an hour, 60 seconds in a minute, and so on. ...The 24 hours...is a curious exception, having derived ... from the Egyptian scheme of dividing the sky longitudinally into 36 time-keeping parts called decans."[1] So we are indebted to the ancient Babylonians and the ancient Egyptians for the counting of our days and their divisions.

Most of us assume that the way our culture or the way that we, ourselves, organize time is the way that time ought to be or at least is organized. In an article entitled "Keeping Sabbath," Dorothy Bass noted, "The way in which time is organized is a fundamental building block of any community. So basic is this that most of us take the pattern we are used to for granted, as if it were self-evident that time must be arranged this way."[2]

But of course, if we remember Henri Nouwen's breakfast experience in Ireland; or have arrived at church services in the Middle East scheduled to begin at, say, 2:00, which may not get underway until 2:30 or 3:00 or later; or have experienced the difference between the way time is treated in the northeastern cities of the United States as opposed to the way it is observed in the deep South, we will know that people treat time differently. To borrow a metaphor from Bruce Malina, time is the dimension of human experience that orients our "mental maps." We learn the temporal orientations favored by our society.³ If we learn them, we can unlearn them. Therein lies our hope that we, too, can change our own view of time, can think about time differently, can "use" or "organize"— or even "receive"— our personal time differently.

The pattern of human life inspires most of us to seek out a rhythm in the time allotted to us. We can observe the physical, emotional, psychological, moral, and spiritual stages of development of children from the earliest sonogram through puberty. Until Gail Sheehy wrote her bestselling book *Passages* several years ago, however, most of us didn't realize that human beings continue to develop and evolve throughout young adulthood, midlife, and elder years in ways that are often predictable. What reassurance it gives us to be enlightened, to know that certain events or symptoms are common or appropriate ("normal") for our season or state in life— and to know that we are not alone, not isolated, not bizarre in an experience or feeling! "To everything a season...."

So too is the need for a rhythm to our days. Most of us have routines even if they are unconscious, even if life seems chaotic. There is comfort in the repetition, in knowing what to expect. The first hour of the day's routine moves us relatively smoothly from unconsciousness to full participation in the day. Usually, the days in the week have a pattern, with daily tasks and pleasures and duties that change from day to day but are repeated week to week (Monday, laundry; Tuesday, ironing; Wednesday, shopping; Thursday, class). When that pattern is disrupted—even for something wonderful like a holiday or a vacation—we can feel ill-at-ease, "off kilter," and out-of-sorts. Part of the stress of moving or changing jobs or having a baby or coming down with a chronic illness is the loss of familiar routines and surroundings, and the need to establish new ones. The most stressful times for me are those when there is no consistency from week to week. I learned this when I moved from a job I'd had for eleven years and discovered that, in the new situation, the week didn't fall into any rhythm. The lack of consistency made me feel harried.

"And on the seventh day God finished the work ... and ... rested on the seventh day from all the work that he had done" (Gen. 2:2). God, Creator and Owner and Giver of time, modeled for all creatures the proper stewardship of this gift of time. Leisure to rest and play, to re-create and to be re-created, is a basic necessity of life. The foundation for the observance of holy time for rest and worship opens the story of humanity and its relationship with God. It is not simply something to be accomplished one particular day of the week. In fact, the need is so deep and so vital that the church has established four ways to pattern time by and for religious purposes; the sabbatical year, the monastic day, the liturgical year, and our heritage from Judaism, Sabbath.

The Sabbatical Year and Jubilee

There is something in the human spirit that longs for a period of rest. We see this longing institutionalized in the communal life of ancient Israel as the sabbatical year. Leviticus 25 gives the fullest account of the sabbatical year. Every seventh year was set aside as a year of restoration for the land.

> When you enter the land that I am giving you, the land shall observe a sabbath for the Lord. Six years you shall sow your field, and six years you shall prune your vineyard, and gather in their yield; but in the seventh year there shall be a sabbath of complete rest for the land, a sabbath for the Lord: you shall not sow your field or prune your vineyard.
> Leviticus 25: 2b-4 and compare Exodus 23:10-11

It was an early, and wise, attempt at ecology. The tacit understanding was that land, and people who work it, wear out and need to be given time to rest. For six years the land was sown and reaped, and in the seventh it was allowed to lie fallow. Left to itself, the land's fertility and ability to support crops was restored.

The principle was carried out in large scale at the fiftieth year, as the "jubilee year" (Lev. 25: 8-17). The fiftieth year was a year of liberty and rest, a year which allowed the righting of the economic balances in ancient Israel so that some of the people would not amass great wealth at the expense of others. Time was structured both to allow for refreshment and to prevent exploitation of natural resources and people. In an April, 1997, article in the magazine *Bible Review* entitled "Jubilee," Jacob Milgrom explored the jubilee year described in Leviticus 25:23-24. jubilee was established to remind ancient Israelites that God is the landlord and they are merely tenant farmers (the reality behind Jesus' parable of the wicked husbandmen in Mark 12:1-11 and parallels). Jubilee years demanded remission of debt, restoration of land, and manumission of slaves, giving Sabbath rest for land and persons and release from economic servitude. This periodic cancellation of debt and return of land blessed and benefited all parties because it prevented the economy from collapsing under the weight of debt. We can find in this ancient practice a realistic blueprint for life in modern societies, a way out of our current economic morass.[4] It is this very idea that Pope John Paul II is advancing when he asks rich nations to cancel the debt of poorer countries for the millennium.

The Monastic Day

Attentiveness to time is one of the hallmarks of monastic life. The day and the year follow a pattern and rhythm designed to maximize attentiveness to God. Since its origins in the third and fourth centuries, Christian monastic life has been especially considerate of the use and misuse of time.

Western monasticism has been most profoundly influenced by Benedict of Nursia (480-547). The guiding principle of the Rule that St. Benedict devised for his monks is a balanced life lived in community. Benedict disapproved of both the extreme austerities that had characterized monastic life and the life of complete solitude which provided no protection for the spiritually overzealous individual. In Benedict's view, the day should be divided among work, study, prayer, and rest in roughly equal proportions. If that balance sounds idyllic, I would encourage you to compare your "Time Log"—and what you learned about how you spend your time—with Benedict's model.

Life in Benedict's monasteries was and is structured around the "Opus Dei," the "work of God," understood as the Divine Office. It consists of periods of formal, oral, communal prayer spaced throughout the day and night. These "offices" of Lauds, Prime, Terce, Sext, None, Vespers, and Compline are made up primarily of recitation of the Psalms, readings from scripture, and hymns. The Office divides the day into portions that are given over to prayer, to work (usually manual work for the sake of the body, with "body" understood as both the monastery community and the physical person of the monk), to study (spiritual reading or conversation), and to rest (both during the day and sleep at night).

This pattern is further shaped by the natural progression of the seasons and by the liturgical year. The Winter Order includes Lent and preparation for Easter. During the Winter Order which begins in September, manual labor is done in the morning and mid-afternoon, with spiritual reading and study before the day's work begins and at its close in the afternoon. The Summer Order begins with Easter and switches work to the early morning hours and late afternoon or early evening when it's cooler, with reading and rest in the mid-day heat. This theological patterning of time is thus directly connected to the natural world and its rhythms.

Benedict's "Rule" suggests that in our Christian tradition great care has been given to how to "spend time."[4] Writing about monastic culture in *The Cloister Walk*, Kathleen Norris notes that "in our culture, time can seem like an enemy: it chews us up and spits us out with appalling ease. But the monastic perspective welcomes time as a gift from God, and seeks to put it to good use rather than allowing us to be used up by it."[6] According to Brother David Steindl-Rast, "Monasticism's central message . . . is the supreme importance of time and how we relate to it: how we care take and respond to the present moment, to what is before us now."[7] The patterning of the monastic day is to help the monk focus on the only time available, now, the present moment.

Between March, 1978, and October, 1979, I was privileged to spend a good deal of time with the Anglican sisters at All Saints Sisters of the Poor convent in Catonsville, Maryland. At the time I was working on a doctoral dissertation on Thomas Merton and discerning life choices. I found the structure the monastic hours gave the day extremely fruitful. The priority was prayer, from which, I discovered, good work naturally flowed. Although I did not embrace vowed monastic life, its priorities and orderliness have exerted a profound influence on me. I am glad to be able to express my gratitude for what I learned. How much more is accomplished when work itself proceeds from prayer and is done by a person who is rested enough to do it! But more important, how much closer we draw to God when we really live in the present moment.

The Liturgical Year

A third approach to measuring time is the church's liturgical year. A year composed of Advent, Christmas, Epiphany, Lent, Easter, Pentecost, and "Ordinary Time" is deeply spiritual, biblical, and Christ-centered. The liturgical year reminds us of God's intersections with human history, that God's pattern is woven through the progression of chronological time, that *chronos* and *kairos* intersect. The liturgical year reminds us that each calendar year is a Year of the Lord; it is deeply christo-logical, following as it does the events in the life of Christ. Each calendar year we are given another opportunity to walk through the life of Jesus, to live again in its scenes and events. Jim Forest, a convert to Orthodoxy, describes the liturgical year as

> . . . a procession of icons through which we keep re-turning to the main events of salvation history. The purpose of the church year, wrote Father Lev Gillet, is not only to bring to the mind of believers the teachings of the Gospel and the main events of Christian history . . . but "to renew and in some sense actualize the event of which it is a symbol, taking the event out of the past and making it immediate." Through the calendar, we begin to see each day as having more than a secular identity but as a door toward closer union with Christ.[8]

In an essay entitled "Time and the Liturgy," Thomas Merton reflects upon the liturgical year this way:

> The liturgy makes the passage of time sanctify our lives, for each new season renews an aspect of the great Mystery of Christ living and present in His Church. Each recurring season shows us some new way in which we live in Him, in which He acts in the world. Each new feast draws our attention to the great truth of His presence in the midst of us, and

shows us a different aspect of the Paschal Mystery in our world.[9]

The liturgical year reminds us that our time is God's time. It keeps us closely in touch with the Incarnation. The seasons themselves suggest a balance for life. There are two quiet, reflective seasons of waiting and preparation, Advent and Lent. There are seasons of great activity and revelation, *kairos* seasons, if you will: Christmas, Epiphany, Easter, Pentecost. And there is the long, slow, "ordinary" time when we are called to reflect upon our own growing life in Christ. "Ordinary time," time when nothing special seems to be going on, is often understood in retrospect to be time of great spiritual growth and deepening. Nancy Meirs has titled one of her books *Ordinary Time* for just this reason. Kathleen Norris reminds us that "liturgical time is essentially poetic time, oriented towards process rather than productivity, willing to wait attentively in stillness rather than always pushing to 'get the job done.'"[10] We Americans in particular, I think, have much to learn from a "process" rather than a "productivity" orientation, and the liturgical year helps us to enter that mode.

The Sabbath

These various ways of patterning time, of punctuating the work day with periods of rest and prayer, of organizing the natural seasons into times of theological remembrance, are grounded in the very story of creation as we preserve it. The Priestly writer who composed Genesis 1:1-2:3 reflects a deep and profound insight into God's ordering of time. God creates light and darkness and then uses that light and darkness, evening and morning, to mark days. "And on the seventh day God finished the work that he had done, and he rested on the seventh day . . . . So God blessed the seventh day and hallowed it, because on it God rested from all his work which he had done in creation" (Gen. 2: 2-3). Genesis tells us quite clearly that God intended for time to be divided between work and rest.

The Babylonian creation myths have many elements in common with our Genesis account, but nothing that clearly parallels God's resting after work. Having created everything, Dorothy Bass notes,

> God rests, and blesses this day, and makes it holy. In this way, Karl Barth has suggested, God declares as fully as possible just how very good creation is. Resting, God takes pleasure in what has been made; God has no regrets, no need to go on to create a still

better world or a creature more wonderful than the man and woman. In the day of rest, God's free love toward humanity takes the form of time shared with them.[11]

One of the marks of Divinity is that God knows when to stop working, when to rest, when to enjoy what has been created by work. Artists tell me that a crucial kind of artistic knowledge is to know when to stop making brush strokes. Arthur Waskow describes it this way:

> There's a moment in painting when you're laying brush stroke after brush stroke . . . and each one's beautiful and each one enhances the painting. Then comes the moment when you put one more brush stroke on and . . . suddenly you have ruined the painting.[12]

We too must learn when to stop. For me, one of the most intriguing aspects of the parable of the Good Samaritan in Luke's gospel has always been that the Samaritan knew when to "stop," when to pay the bill and move on. I think a mark of our distance from God and from Godliness and from our reality as creatures made in God's image is that we often do not know when to stop. We keep working until it is counterproductive. In fact, we have found it hard to take seriously God's command to rest. And it *is* a command, not a polite request. The writer of Exodus gives us not only the commandment, but commentary on it.

Remember the sabbath day, to keep it holy. Six days you shall labor, and do all your work. But the seventh day is a sabbath to the Lord your God; you shall not do any work—you, or your son or your daughter, your male or female slave, your livestock, or the alien resident in your towns. For in six days the Lord made heaven and earth, the sea, and all that is in them, but rested the seventh day; therefore the Lord blessed the sabbath day and consecrated it.

Exodus 20:8–11

God is so gracious to us that God has commanded us to rest. The Hebrew word for "rest" literally means "to catch your breath." God has commanded us to "take time" to catch our breath and to give those who live and work with us the opportunity to do the same.

We have not obeyed God's commandment, we have not conformed our schedules to this fourth, most basic, rhythm of time, and the consequences have been serious. In the 1991 bestseller *The Overworked American*, economist Juliet Schor's research suggests that work hours and stress are on the rise and that sleep and family time are on the decline for all classes of working Americans. Her conclusion is that we live in a society that is demanding too much of people. Similarly, Arlie Hochschild's 1997 book *The Time Bind* says we work too much not because we have to, but because we want to. Hochschild's research concludes with the troubling notion that we like it better at work than at home. We hardly needed these research projects to tell us we work too much. We know it in our own bodies. We know it among our friends. We all know too many overextended people who suffer from depression and stress illnesses. Neither parents nor chief executives, neither ministers nor those who are unemployed, neither monks nor vowed Religious are exempt.

It should be abundantly clear that it is long past time for us to recover the theology and practice of the Sabbath. According to Dorothy Bass, "We need Sabbath, even though we doubt that we have time for it."[13] If we refresh our memories about the biblical origins of Sabbath, its observance and purpose in Israel's life, then we might have faith that the suggestions in the next chapter will help us find ways in which we might all recover a viable Sabbath practice.

The idea of Sabbath time actually predates our biblical Hebrews. In ancient Babylon there is evidence of a distinctive day called *sabattu*. It was specifically designated as the "day of quieting the heart," and while the exact meaning of this phrase isn't clear, it resonates deeply and certainly connotes some concept of inner relaxation. The word is probably identical with the Hebrew, *Sabbath*, which comes from a verbal root meaning "to cease, to abstain, to desist from, to terminate, to be at an end."[14] The connotation "rest" for the noun actually was introduced in the post-biblical period.

In Hebrew scripture Sabbath is a defining practice of Israel from her earliest days. Sabbath originated with the creation itself and appears in all the major law codes. It's prominent in the prophetic writings. Sabbath as a communal practice probably originated in the agricultural period of Israel's history (after the Conquest). From a day upon which labor was strictly prohibited, in the post-Exilic period, it came to have a much more positive connotation. Sabbath became a day of rest and relaxation, a day of high and divinely given privilege for Israel and all those under her care on any given Sabbath—foreigners, travelers, slaves, and even animals, a privilege to be extended to all people. With his characteristic universalizing vision, the prophet Isaiah wrote, "From new moon to new moon, and from sabbath to sabbath, / all flesh shall come to worship before me, / says the Lord" (Is. 66:23). Given as a gift to Israel, Isaiah declared, God intended Sabbath time be extended to all people, all flesh.

In the biblical record, Sabbath is the sign of God's sanctification of Israel as God's people and of God's eternal covenant with her. Through the prophet Ezekiel God declared, "I gave them my sabbaths, as a sign between me and them, so that they might know that I the Lord sanctify them" (Ez. 20:12, cf. Ex. 31:13). From all the nations, God chose Israel alone to observe Sabbath in God's honor. Sabbath was to be observed in joyous celebration and appreciation for the privilege of worshipping God. "If you refrain from trampling the sabbath, / from pursuing your own interests on my holy day; / if you call the Sabbath a delight and the holy day of the Lord honorable;/ if you honor it, not going your own ways, serving your own interests, or pursuing your own affairs; / then you shall take delight in the Lord, / and I will make you ride upon the heights of the earth . . ." (Is. 58:13-14)[15] Sabbath had the theological purpose of memorializing God's resting from the work of creation and of reminding people of their special relationship to God, and the practical purpose of giving people and animals a time of rest.

The New Testament suggests that Jewish Christians continued to observe Sabbath, but Gentile Christians gradually moved from Saturday, the last day of the week, to Sunday, the first day of the week, as their day of commemoration. According to Biblical tradition, God created light on the first day, and Jesus, the light of the world, was raised from the dead on the first day of the week. So Sabbath practice gradually became the observance of Sunday.[16] The Epistle of Barnabas, a Christian letter from the end of the first or the beginning of the second century, devotes a chapter to the Sabbath and speaks of the beginning of an eighth day which Christians celebrate with gladness as the "day in which Jesus also rose from the dead, and was made manifest, and ascended into Heaven" (15:9). Today Orthodox Christians view Pascha (Easter) as the eighth day of the week and every Sunday is a "little Pascha."[17]

Christians may not need to return to the observance of the seventh day of the week as the Sabbath. But the concept of Sabbath, its origin and intention, needs to be reclaimed by all people, for our own good. There is, as Tilden Edwards points out in his book *Sabbath Time,* a basic human need for a different quality of time than that which we experience in the daily routine of our lives.[18] We need holidays, that expression which is a corruption of "holy days." Sabbath time is of enormous physical and spiritual value to us. It is a reminder of God's benevolence in creation, of our chosenness as God's creatures. And it is a gracious corrective to American (and perhaps all Western) Christianity's besetting sin: "works-righteousness". We can stop working and the universe will go chugging along quite nicely because it is, after all, God, and not our activity, who keeps it in motion. We desperately need what the writer of the Hebrew letter calls the "Sabbath rest [that] still remains for the people of God" (Heb. 4:9) for our spiritual and for our physical well being.

In his wonderful book on the Sabbath, Rabbi Abraham Heschel says that we must "learn to understand that the world has already been created and will survive without the help of man. Six days a week we wrestle with the world, wringing profit from the earth; on the Sabbath we especially care for the seed of eternity planted in the soul."[19] The Sabbath is a day for the sake of life, he continues, the seventh day "is a palace in time which we build."[20] Sabbath is about recovering holiness in time, about bringing the seed of eternity to flowering, about converting time into eternity, about being in love with eternity. Sabbath is a "realm of time where the goal is not to have but to be, not to own but to give, not to control but to share, not to subdue but to be in accord."[21] These are the high aspirations of authentic and mature Christian life: to be, to give, to share, to be in accord.

Edwards speaks of the Christian Sabbath, of Sunday (although "Sabbath time" can occur on any day of the week), as "...potentially an intimate realization of the coinherence of human and divine time, and an opportunity to surrender our little time to God's enormous time for transformation. Sabbath is a structured opportunity to realize the relativity of our time in God's time."[22] Edwards understands that realistically in our day and age Sabbath time doesn't just "happen." In 321 A.D. the Emperor Constantine made Sunday a day of rest throughout the Roman Empire. That was a long time ago; we are certainly in another era. Gone are the Blue Laws that closed business and thus slowed Americans down on Sundays. We are going to have to "make" or "take" time for Sabbath so that we can "spend" time with God. For this is the ultimate purpose of Sabbath time, to be with God, to use human time to open up space for God.

One of the great Christian hopes is that we will spend eternity with God. If that is the case, shouldn't we be intentional now about getting to know the One with

Whom we will be spending eternity? Why are we so afraid to do this? Why do we have to be so busy all the time? I was startled when one of my colleagues at Pittsburgh Seminary preached on what he called the "bitch/brag syndrome." You know it. The conversation goes like this: "How are you?" "Oh, I'm just SO busy. . .," followed by a list of all the things the person thinks she needs to do. Beneath the complaint that we are too busy, that we don't have any time, is really the pride of attainment. "I'm so busy" may well be a way of saying, "See how needed I am, see how important I am." Whom are we trying to convince? If busy-ness is about pride of attainment, we are spiritually on very thin ice, indeed, for we are dangerously close to what I referred to before as "works righteousness."

Nothing I "do" ultimately assures my value. My value as a human being is already secured by God as the source of my creation and by Jesus Christ as the source of my salvation. I may choose to engage in "good works"—benevolence, charity, whatever—as a grateful response to those gifts, but there is absolutely nothing I could do to earn them. The bottom line is I don't have to do anything; I just have to be, that is, to accept God's gift of life and to respond by grateful living. Why is it that this Christian ontology is so hard to accept? Could it be because the nature of God is so foreign to us? We do not deeply, existentially, understand that God is Love, that God loves us because that is God's nature, not because we are smart or pretty or productive or "worthy" of such love. Because human love so rarely comes to us unconditionally, many of us have decided that God's love never could either. We are wrong in this assumption, as the cross of Jesus Christ so clearly demonstrates.

My point is really quite simple and self-evident. Time is given to us by God. We can steward it if we choose; we can create, or more precisely, mirror the sacred rhythms in our own time. Usually we don't. We work too much and rest too little. Our besetting sin is overwork. What we need is to recover a profoundly biblical concept, a concept which, in fact, is given by our gracious God as a command—that of Sabbath. We need to make "structured opportunities" for Sabbath time, for times of rest with God and God's people. In the next chapter, I will suggest some practical ways we might do that. But first, let us recall some words of encouragement and challenge.

Although the exclusivity of its language will be difficult for some readers, two stanzas of the hymn by John G. Whittier (1807-1892), "Dear Lord and Father of Mankind," express with great clarity the need that we have for Sabbath time:

> O Sabbath rest by Galilee!
> O calm of hills above
> Where Jesus knelt to share with thee
> The silence of eternity,
> Interpreted by love!

Drop thy still dews of quietness,
Till all our strivings cease;
Take from our souls the strain and stress,
And let our ordered lives confess
The beauty of thy peace.

The hymn reminds us that Jesus, Himself, needed Sabbath, needed and took time to withdraw to be with God alone, to enter into the "silence of eternity," the radically altered quality of Divine time. We need this, too. We need the "dews of quietness," and we can receive them more fully when we order our lives to be available to them. The suggestion is that "ordered lives" are more peaceful and less strained and stressful. My own experiences of monastic communities and relationships with people in religious life bears this out.

I've also discovered an appreciation for a beautiful and suggestive word in studying Matthew's gospel with theology students. Three times in the central section of Matthew Jesus is described as "withdrawing." The Greek verb for "withdraw" is *anachoreo*. Its lectionary definition is "to withdraw," "to go away," and "to return." It is a compound word made up of *ana*, in Greek "each" or "each one," and *choreo*, literally "to make room for." The suggestion is that in "withdrawing" for times of Sabbath, or of rest and prayer, we are literally making room for each of the persons and situations we will encounter when we return.

The writer of the Book of Hebrews reminds us that God still offers us a Sabbath rest. "A sabbath rest still remains for the people of God; for those who enter God's rest also cease from their labors as God did from his. Let us therefore make every effort to enter that rest. . ." (Heb. 4:9-11). The Sabbath rest is there, but it may require some effort on our part to enter it. We are nevertheless invited to do so. In fact, we are invited to do so by our Lord, Jesus Christ. "Come to me, all you that are weary and are carrying heavy burdens, and I will give you rest. Take my yoke upon you, and learn from me; for I am gentle and humble in heart, and you will find rest for your souls" (Mt. 11:28-29). His words are not only invitation, but promise. Certainly it is "time" to embrace both.

SIX

"A Sabbath Rest for the People of God"

The Sabbath was made for humankind, not humankind for the Sabbath.

—Mark 2:27

From an ad for a luxury wrist watch, the words of the great opera singer Dame Kiri Te Kanawa's endorsement surely resonate with most of us: "Time … just gets more and more precious." Considering just how valuable time is, we might ask with a certain degree of (understandable!) avarice, "How can I have more of it?" Is there a way to redeem (from the Latin word *redimere*, a composite of *re*, meaning back, and *emere*, to get) the time allotted to us, to get back or set free or rescue time?

The collect for Saturday from the Daily Office of the Episcopal Church reminds us of the importance of a day of rest.

> Almighty God, who after the creation of the world rested from all your works and sanctified a day of rest for all your creatures: Grant that we, putting away all earthly anxieties, may be duly prepared for the service of your sanctuary, and that our rest upon earth may be a preparation for the eternal rest you promised your people in heaven; through Jesus Christ our Lord. AMEN.[1]

The prayer reflects the fact that God has sanctified, made holy, a day of rest for *all* creatures, not just human beings. This would have been crucial in Israel's agricultural period, when healthy, rested animals meant fruitful work, but it reminds us that we humans are charged to provide rest for all God's creatures. The collect goes on to suggest that on this day we should "put away all earthly anxiety" (that, in itself, is a wonderfully refreshing thought) in order to be "prepared for the service of [God's] sanctuary."

Notice that the day of Christian rest is not Sunday. The implication is that Saturday, the historic Sabbath, is given over to rest in order to prepare us Christians for the worship of God on Sunday. And this earthly rest is the preparation for eternal rest. If we don't learn to rest here on earth, there are going to be some pretty antsy folks in heaven! A Larson cartoon makes just this point. A bored-looking angel sitting on a fluffy cloud says, "Wish I'd brought a magazine."

The Saturday collect puts into sharp focus some very

important aspects of Sabbath time. It asks us to be willing to suspend earthly concerns for the purpose of being ready to worship God both now and forever. As Sister Joan Chittister, O.S.B., noted in a talk entitled "Recovering Lost Sabbath," Sabbath calls us "to worship what deserves to be worshipped and to dismiss from the center of our souls what does not."[2]

Before we explore those ideas in a little more depth, let us recall that the concept of Sabbath time was of great importance to Jesus himself. We all know the stories in which He broke the Sabbath in order to address human need. Early in Mark's gospel, for example, Jesus feeds his disciples (2:23-28) and heals a man with a withered hand (3:1-6) on the Sabbath. Those accounts warn us against religious legalism of any kind. Specifically, they announce "The sabbath was made for humankind, and not humankind for the sabbath" (Mk 2:27). This is an important saying, and it goes far beyond a condemnation of narrow legalism. Jesus is stating unequivocally that the Sabbath was made as a gift for human beings. Sabbath is part of God's gracious provision for us; it was created for our benefit.

I am not seeking to impose another "rule to be followed" in asking us to consider "making Sabbath." In fact, the life of Jesus suggests to us that "Sabbath time" need not occur on the seventh day of the week. Jesus, in fact, was "making Sabbath" in the sense that I am commending it on all those occasions when we see Him withdrawing for prayer (Mk. 1:35, 6:46), an activity which is characteristic of Luke's Jesus in particular. (See for example, Lk. 3:21, 4:42, 5:16, 6:12, 9:10, 9:18, 11:1.) Jesus also reminds his disciples of their own need to "come away" for a bit (Mk. 6:31). Even as He shows us that pressing human need might require that we give up THE Sabbath, the seventh day of the calendar week, in order to serve others or to meet legitimate needs, "making Sabbath" is part of the example that Jesus sets for us in his own life of engagement and withdrawal. In fact, Sabbath as a time to "watch and pray" constitutes practically the last teaching of Jesus to his disciples in the "apocalyptic discourse" in Mark 13: 33, 37, and it is the one they ignore to their great shame and peril in the Garden of Gethsemane (Mk. 14:34, 38).

Perhaps the hardest obstacle to be overcome in our "making Sabbath time" is the obstacle of what the collect called "putting away earthly anxiety." How hard it is for us to set aside the things we worry about! And, truthfully, many of us worry about important things: peace, justice, family concerns, health. How especially hard it is for those of us who are in the helping professions—ministers, health professionals, therapists, teachers—to set aside our work! It is, after all, *important* work. People's lives depend upon it. But if we are overextended and exhausted, what do we have to give people? Without Sabbath time, sooner or later (probably sooner) we will "burn out."

This is yet another reason why we might resist the idea of Sabbath time. It forces us to consider the nature of our attitude toward work. If we can't stop working, it may well be that we have *become* our work; that is, that we have tied our identities so closely to what we *do* that without that doing we doubt the value of our existence. This is very dangerous spiritually, indeed. It is why losing a job is so traumatic to some people. It is why "retirement age" looms so menacingly for some. It's not just that the source of livelihood is in jeopardy with job loss or retirement; the more serious issue is that the sense of *self* is diminished.

Sabbath requires that we ask important questions about the nature of the self. In *New Seeds of Contemplation,* Thomas Merton reflected a great deal on what he called the "true" and "false" self. The "false self," he argued, exists in our egocentric desires. We often think of it as "the fundamental reality of life to which everything else in the universe is ordered."

> Thus I use up my life in the desire for pleasures and the thirst for experiences, for power, honor, knowledge and love, to clothe this false self and construct its nothingness into something objectively real. And I wind experiences around myself . . . in order to make myself perceptible to myself and to the world . . . .
>
> But there is no substance under the things with which I am clothed. I am hollow, and my structure

of pleasures and ambitions has no foundation. I am objectified in them. But they are all destined by their very contingency to be destroyed. And when they are gone there will be nothing left of me but my own nakedness and emptiness and hollowness . . . . [3]

Some of us may resist the notion of Sabbath time because it forces us to face painful issues of our own identity before God. Sabbath time encourages us to ask the question posed in an earlier exercise, "Who am I when I'm not doing what I do?" It is an important question, one that may help lead us to our true self, the one which Merton tells us "is hidden in the love and mercy of God."[4]

In writing about the great impact of the Puritans on American Sunday practice in the early centuries of our country, Tilden Edwards noted that for them "the primary purpose of life was seen as furthering the divine purpose through our particular callings."[5] (Remember here my own perception of time—that I believe God will grant me the time necessary to accomplish what God needs of me. That gives me "enough" time.) The purpose of life is to further the Divine Purposes, not to advance our careers or make more money or even provide more security for our families. At its core, Christian life is a profound cooperation with the plans and purposes of God. That puts a rather different spin on the matter of our work life and on Sabbath time, since Sabbath seems so clearly to be part of God's purpose for God's people. In his book, *The Sabbath,* Abraham Heschel suggests that the higher goal of spiritual living is to "face sacred moments."[6] By keeping Sabbath, he notes, we affirm the value of work, but we also "stop worshipping the idols of technical civilization."[7] Both Sister Joan Chittister and Rabbi Heschel suggest that Sabbath helps us keep clearly in mind Who is to be worshipped. The suggestion is thus strong that our inability to find time for Sabbath rest is, at worst, a form of idolatry and, at best, putting our own agendas before God's.

Why are we so unwilling to set aside Sabbath time? Does it have to do with an un-holy attitude toward work that is the outward and visible manifestation of a deeply flawed understanding of the locus of value of the human person? Does it have to do with our fear of facing ourselves or of facing "sacred moments"? If I stay busy enough, I can probably avoid both myself and God. But should I? It is at best a temporary ploy, for one day each one of us will have to face God and give an accounting of ourselves and our gifts, including our use of time.

The Saturday collect also suggested that Sabbath time was really to prepare us for worship both on earth and in heaven. Worship is not to be entered into lightly or without preparation. I always want to ask the folks who complain to me that worship is boring or unsatisfying, "What did you do to prepare for it and how did you participate in it?" It's the aspect of preparation that is relevant here.

If we race into church on Sunday morning, weary from a short night's sleep after staying up too late on Saturday in frenetic activity and anxious about the list of things we have to do Sunday afternoon and evening, we are unlikely to be able, much less prepared, to worship. Authentic worship of God can spring from many sources in human life, but one is certainly from Sabbath time, from a time of rest and of "letting go," from a deep, existential conviction that there is enough time for it because time for us is part of God's gift.

A Christian theology of time, as we have noted, would certainly understand the idea that time and eternity are intrinsically related. For Christians, time moves into eternity. This is why it's possible for earthly worship to be a preparation for heavenly worship of the sort that St. John envisioned around the throne of the Lamb in the book of Revelation—see, for example, chapters four and five of that book. Heschel says that "The Sabbath is an example of the world to come. . . . Unless one learns how to relish the taste of Sabbath while still in this world, unless one is initiated in the appreciation of eternal life, one will be unable to enjoy the taste of eternity in the world to come."[8] In short, Sabbath is an "acquired taste," one that prepares the spiritual taste buds for heaven. In my experience, a small taste, carefully savored, creates a great appetite for it. We should "look to the Sabbath as our homeland, our source and destination."[9] That is because Sabbath time, properly understood, keeps us in touch with God Who Is our Source and Destination.

As Orthodox Christianity maintains, worship, itself, is a making of Sabbath. Jim Forest writes that in "…Orthodoxy the Liturgy truly orders us to rest from our worries."[10] About midway in the liturgy, the stately Cherubic Hymn enjoins, "Let us who mystically represent the Cherubim . . . now lay aside all earthly care." Even learning to pray in the unhurried way of the great liturgies like those of St. John Chrysostom can help people to become less hurried. In a general way, "taking time" for prayer is, itself, "making Sabbath."

Time and the Eucharist

The Saturday collect with which this chapter began pointed out that on Sabbath we put away earthly anxiety so that we "may be duly prepared for the service of your sanctuary." That "service" has traditionally been understood by the church catholic to be the Eucharist. Historically, the church has gathered on the first day of the week to celebrate the Lord's Supper, to participate in the Eucharist, our great thanksgiving feast. And this is especially important to developing a spirituality of time because time is so focal in understanding the Eucharist.

I am a product of two Christian communities which have built their communal lives and liturgies around the Eucharist: the Christian Church (Disciples of Christ) and the Episcopal or Anglican traditions. From my earliest childhood, Sunday has been focused around participating in the Lord's Supper. It was around Christ's Table that the hopes and fears, the aspirations and disappointments of my family and friends were sanctified. As I have matured, that Table has become central in my own life as well. Here I gather not only with Christians in my own geographic community, but with all Christians who are celebrating Eucharist, both on earth and in heaven. And this is because time is experienced at Eucharist differently than in any other circumstance.

Hans Reichenbach opens his book *The Direction of Time* this way:

> It appears as though the flow of time, which orders the events of the physical world, passes through human consciousness and compels it to adjust itself to the same order. Our observations of physical things, our feelings and emotions, and our thinking processes extend through time and cannot escape the steady current that flows unhaltingly from the past by way of the present to the future.[11]

At the Eucharist, we can (and do) "escape the steady current that flows unhaltingly"; we step outside time's "ever rolling stream." At the Eucharist, time collapses in on itself. Or to return to language I have used earlier in this study, all time—past, present, future—is contained in the present moment.

If time is a function of Divine disclosure and the "medium for God's saving acts,"[12] then time takes on a special character at the Lord's Table. God entered time in the person of Jesus of Nazareth, took it into the Divine self, redeemed it and filled it with intimations of eternity. After the resurrection, time and eternity co-inhere in wonderful and mysterious ways as the sacraments become "prolongations of Christ's redemptive presence"[13] in human time.

This is especially true at the Eucharist. The Lord's Supper is an event in the present that proclaims an event from the past which assures our future. It is a moment when Jesus is present with the church. For Roman Catholics, the crucified-and-risen Christ Jesus is in fact present in the Eucharist. A catechetical text from the Orthodox tradition describes the matter as follows:

> The eucharist allows us to escape chronological, historical time, the succession of days, hours, and minutes. It allows us to live everything at once: the past, the present, and the future. For liturgical time is not subject to linear time. It allows us to know the eternity of God, where "the past, the present, and the future somehow mysteriously coexist, where the 'already' and the 'not yet' meet one another."[14]

At the Lord's Table all of time is mystically present in a moment of time. Past becomes present and future.[15] At the Eucharist, time opens out into timelessness, and this is another reason why Christians are closer to God at the Eucharist than at any other "time."

At the Eucharist, Christians recall the past in at least three ways. We remember the historical Jesus, the past of the Christian Church, and our own, private lives. And by that means we are reunited with those who are no longer physically present with us in the "now," but who are with us in the Church that includes what the writer of Hebrews calls "the great cloud of witnesses" (12:1), the "communion of saints." And as we remember the living Church in sharing the symbols of the death of Jesus, it is also re-membered, reunited with, all who were in the past and who are in the present and who will be in Christ's final Kingdom. Past becomes present and future.

At the Eucharist, Christians experience the present as God's call to action in their own day, "now." We "proclaim" (present tense) the central event of our faith. We experience the Risen Christ with us and a living union with all Christians in our era in history who observe this Lord's Supper, even if this union must remain a mystical intuition rather than the actual reality of shared Eucharistic celebration. Our present is strengthened by our past for the future.

Finally, at the Lord's Table, Christians receive a foretaste of what it will be like in the Kingdom. We look forward with anticipation to the return of Christ and the cosmic redemption, redress, and rejuvenation that event promises. Our liturgy proclaims, "As often as we eat this bread and drink this cup, we proclaim the Lord's death until He comes." We look forward with great joy to that event and the full reunion it will bring with the saints who have gone on before us (and who, we hope, await with joy our coming). And we look forward to the full reception of our personal inheritance as sons and daughters of God when we are invited to join with the redeemed creation at His Table in the Kingdom. And then the past and the future will be forever present, fully redeemed.

In one of the most deeply moving reflections on time that I know, T.S. Eliot's *Four Quartets,* something of this co-inherence of time is expressed. I urge you to ponder the depth of Eliot's understanding of time, and the wonderment of his attempts to capture the most mysterious of truths—that all the seasons of time (past, present, and future) are all present in each state; that the "points" of time—"beginnings" and "endings"—are endlessly simultaneous, never linear; that in every beginning is an end and in every end, a beginning; and most arrestingly of all—that the culmination of our life's journey "will be to arrive where we started / and to know the place for the first time."[16]

Exercise: Making Sabbath

For theological and spiritual, as well as for health and physical reasons, it is in our own best interests to "make Sabbath." But how, practically, can busy people like us do it? As Dorothy Bass has noted, for many of us, receiving the gift of God that Sabbath time is ". . .will require first discarding our image of Sabbath as a time of negative rules and restrictions, as a day of obligation (for Catholics) or a day without play (in memories of strict Protestant childhoods)."[17] Sabbath time is to be viewed as a joy, as a celebration, as a time of great pleasure. Sabbath time is not to be endured as an obligation, but celebrated as a gift and an opportunity.

For clergy and lay ministers and perhaps for many others, Sabbath time may not fall on Sunday (although Sunday afternoon may offer some possibility). If Sunday cannot be our day of rest and prayer, we need to set aside other times of the week and of the year to function for us as Sabbath time. God's ideal for us is that we set aside Sabbath time weekly, one full day in every seven. If a person were to devote one-seventh of his or her time to Sabbath, that person would have fifty-two Sabbath days a year and about ten years of Sabbath rest in a lifetime![18] I would remind you that this seems to have been the Divine Plan for human life. It is well documented, for example, what happened after the French Revolution when the Republicans tried to institute a nine-day week. Good stewardship would suggest that if we tithe our money (a practice sadly out of fashion, I know), we ought to give at least one-seventh of our time to our relationship to God. In other words, we owe it to God and to ourselves to rescue, to redeem—or more precisely, to *accept*—one-seventh of our time as pure gift of God to be used for rest and worship, both broadly understood.

How might a person do this? At the beginning of the year, I mark off in my calendar one day a week or one morning and one afternoon or two afternoons or an afternoon and an evening as our weekly "Sabbath time." Or perhaps your life changes, by quarters or semesters— then reserve your "Sabbath time" at the beginning of that designated period of time. Each January I mark off one weekend a month as a more "extended Sabbath" to remind myself to keep some time free. I save two long weekends, one in fall and one in spring, for short, quiet retreats, and I reserve one week in the summer for a longer retreat.

Sometimes life and responsibilities intrude on these plans. Sometimes I make a choice to "violate Sabbath," by accepting a speaking engagement or a social invitation in the "marked off" periods. Sometimes my responsibilities as teacher/pastor/author/friend/family member compete with my responsibility to keep the Sabbath. But at least I've set before myself the importance of Sabbath time even if I can't always accept it; I've acknowledged the need to redeem some time, to "save" time to nurture my inner life and my relationship with God. The point is that if we are going to have Sabbath time, we're going to have to be intentional about it, to "structure the opportunity." It won't happen unless we plan it, just as our tithe doesn't happen unless we set it aside first before we pay the bills.

You might need to begin the process on a smaller scale. My friend Sister Marian, who knows me well and knows my besetting sin is overwork, reminds me to take "minute vacations." By this she means to pause in the midst of work to remind myself of God's presence and to be refreshed. A "minute vacation" might mean leaving your desk for a few moments to enjoy the blue sky seen from the window, to have a cup of tea, or to listen to soothing music. It might mean giving yourself permission to put off a chore until tomorrow in order to have a long soak in the tub or a walk in a park or garden. Giving ourselves "minute vacations" can be the appetizer that leads to a desire for full Sabbath "meals."

Once we are able to set the time aside—which, in spite of what it may sound like, may be the easiest part of the process—what do we "do" or what do we "not do" during our Sabbath times? In *Anam Cara,* John O'Donohue quotes the Polish poet Tadeusz Rozewica, who says, "It is more difficult to spend a day well than to write a book." O'Donohue continues, "A day is precious because each day is essentially the microcosm of your whole life."[19] Sabbath days are especially difficult in one sense because we load them with so much expectation. We carry all the "oughts" and "shoulds" of spending them well. But if a Sabbath day is a microcosm of the whole life, all that is really "required" of us is that we be attentive to and in the presence of God. Personally, I admit that I have trouble at this point. My tendency is to want to "accomplish" during Sabbath time: I want to *do* things—to accomplish prayer, to accomplish spiritual reading. I suspect I am not the only one who hasn't got the balance worked out correctly yet, but I do understand, at least in theory, some principles about what should and shouldn't happen in Sabbath time.

The first principle has to do with the reckoning of time itself. I once heard Dr. Henry Mitchell preach. He began by lamenting the "tyranny of time in the abstract," and at the outset of his sermon he asked each of us in the congregation to remove our wrist watches. It wasn't an easy thing to do, and that, in itself, made an important point. Dare I suggest that the first thing we need to do in our Sabbath times is to take off our wrist watches? "Making Sabbath" requires that we reattune ourselves to the rhythms of the natural world and to our own bodies. Why not eat when we are hungry or sleep when we are weary rather than worrying about whether it's "time" to do so? Why not let the activities that we have chosen, or the lack of them, "fill" the time naturally? Sabbath times probably ought to be unscheduled times, times when we are not following a carefully planned itinerary based on the arbitrary hands of our watches and clocks. It's good for our perspective to realize that most of the people in the world have neither.

The second thing to keep in mind during our Sabbath time is that we must not "work," however we conceive of that. In the Orthodox Jewish tradition, people are forbidden from even thinking of business or of work or of planning in regard to them on the Sabbath. That is because Sabbath time as a time of rest, of giving our spirits time to catch up, "is not for the purpose of recovering one's lost strength and becoming fit for the forthcoming labor. The Sabbath is a day for the sake of life. Man is not a beast of burden, and the Sabbath is not for the purpose of enhancing the efficiency of his work. . . . The Sabbath is not for the sake of the weekdays; the weekdays are for the sake of Sabbath. It is not an interlude but the climax of living."[20] Work and commerce and worry are not good on the Sabbath. "To act as if the world cannot get along without our work for one day in seven is a startling display of pride that denies the sufficiency of our generous Maker."[21] So, as Edwards points out, *using* Sabbath time "as preparation for something else, even for something good, is but another inadequate motive that will prevent full resting in the Lord."[22]

What should be encouraged during our Sabbath times are rest and an attitude of restfulness, listening, "wasting time with God," doing nothing. O'Donohue suggests:

> Giving yourself plenty of time is a simple but vital reflective exercise: Leave all agendas behind you. Let the neglected presence of your soul come to meet and engage you again. It can be a lovely reacquaintance with your forgotten mystery.[23]

Our Sabbath might include long hours of sleep, time in solitude, time for prayer and worship, reading, listening to music. It might include time outside, walking, gardening, enjoying the natural world. I hesitate to suggest engagement in sports because of the attitude of competition that so often goes along with it. The need to "win" at golf or tennis, for example, often puts us in the same competitive "work" mentality that Sabbath time is to liberate us from! Sabbath time might include family time, preparation of special meals together, visiting. Sabbath time is for experiencing delight in the goodness of life and of the Giver of that life, and so it naturally includes rest, play, eating, the "good things of life." There is no need to be guilty about any of this; it is what God intends for us. In addressing various kinds of abstinence, the writer of 1 Timothy puts it extravagantly. "For everything created by God is good, and nothing is to be rejected, provided it is received with thanksgiving" (1 Tim. 4:4).

One of the things Sabbath time can do for us is to re-

connect us with the primary source of joy, which is gratitude. As Esther de Waal writes, "The generosity of God
in sharing the goodness of creation with us can elicit only
one possible response—that of gratitude."[24] Joy blossoms
in gratitude for what we have been given, beginning with
the gift of life itself. Gratitude is the proper response of
the creature to the Creator—his or her very origin is gift!
"The root of joy is gratefulness," writes Brother David
Steindl-Rast in *Gratefulness: The Heart of Prayer*, "and
gratefulness is the measure of our aliveness."[25] Sabbath
gives us time to remember our origins, to revitalize our
connection to the joy that gives life.

To return, then, to the matter at hand. What about
Sabbath time and the demands of family life? Tilden Edwards, director of the Shalem Institute in Washington,
D.C., explains that his family has kept Sabbath for years.
Yes, that family includes children. Part IV of his book
Sabbath Time provides ample practical advice about how
to "make Sabbath." From his long years of Sabbath practice he suggests that for most of us Sabbath time and
Sabbath rest involve two stages. The first is "letting go,"
putting aside our normal routines and work. This he calls
the "external stage" of Sabbath time. It's the blocking
out of those days in the calendar. The second stage is
"letting ourselves be" in Sabbath time. This is the "inter-
nal stage" and involves our attitude and alertness and
focus of attention *in* Sabbath.[26] This is what happens
when we leave behind our doing and rest in being in

God. For most of us, this takes some practice and a great deal of "letting be."

Without falling into a legalistic trap by implying that there is a right and wrong way to make Sabbath, let us ask ourselves how we might make Sabbath in the way God intended for us, specifically. How we find that time and what we fill it with will be highly individual, as deeply personal as our pattern and form of prayer. The following questions might help you think about how you and your family can "make Sabbath":

1. How can I "find" time for Sabbath? What odds and ends of time might be used for Sabbath focus? Does my work situation allow me some time off? a sabbatical? "mental health" days? Can I begin immediately to take "minute vacations"?

2. What sorts of activities might be appropriate for Sabbath time? What things do I do that put me in touch with God? What things distance me from the Divine dimension of life? What gives me energy? What drains me? As I approach the idea of Sabbath time, what do I experience as my own "needs" both physical and spiritual? How are both related to openness to God?

3. What are the practical issues to be faced in my family and my situation as I/we approach making Sabbath? How can this be a positive experience for all of us? How can I "make Sabbath" if the rest of my family is uninterested in the idea? How can I/we meet objections to our "wasting time" in this way?

Time, properly understood, gratefully accepted, wisely spent, will bring us to the end of our time, knowing with quiet conviction that it is where we began and where we begin again, forever.

SEVEN

No Time Like the Present

> This is the day that the Lord has made; let us rejoice and be glad in it.
>
> —Psalm 118:24

If we return to our starting point for this reflection on time, John O'Donohue's *Anam Cara*, you might suspect that the title of this chapter is, in some measure, ironic. Consider his observations:

> Time and again, we miss out on the great treasures in our lives because we are so restless. In our minds we are always elsewhere. We are seldom in the place where we stand and in the time that is now. Many people are haunted by the past, things that they have not done, things that they should have done that they regret not doing. They are prisoners of their past. Other people are haunted by the future; they are anxious and worried about what is coming.[1]

The expression "No time like the present" implies a zest for life in the moment, doing and savoring now. But in fact, most Americans do not really live in the present, much less have a *carpe diem*, "seize-the-day" sort of enthusiasm about what is. (But we like it when we see it, as in the movie "Dead Poets Society.") To show that Mediterranean peasants of the first century experienced time differently from modern people and to demonstrate the relevance of that fact for New Testament interpretation, Bruce Malina points out that "mainstream, middle class America is future-oriented. People live achievement-directed lives focused on relatively distant goals. They work and act in the present in order in some way to realize some far off purpose. . . . The present always serves as a means to some more distant end."[2]

Unfortunately, I think both O'Donohue and Malina are correct in their respective analyses. Many of us, at least internally, do not live in the here-and-now. We are consumed with what was or with what might have been, or we are worried about what will or what might be. As Malina notes, we can't even take satisfaction in our work in the present because it is for some future end (a college education, a bigger house or car, a retirement income). And when we consider time from the standpoint of life in the spirit, this is a terrible danger. I would go so far as to say that a great deal of the spiritual anguish we experience is because we are not content to be, to live in the present, simply to enjoy the riches of existence in the here-and-now. No wonder we feel harried. We are of the present, but not in it.

This is a particularly precarious position for Christians. Our New Testament, and especially the gospels, is remarkably present-oriented. Matthew's Jesus says, "Do not worry about tomorrow, for tomorrow will bring worries of its own. Today's trouble is enough for today" (Mt. 6:34). Luke's Jesus declares, "The kingdom of God *is not coming* with things that can be observed. . . . For, in fact, the kingdom of God *is among* [or *within*] you" (Lk. 17:20, 21; italics mine). Jesus teaches His disciples to pray for their *daily* bread. (Mt. 6:11; Lk 11:3 *Pace* to the problems of translating *epiousion* from the Greek into English.) It is hard to overlook the fact that in Mark's gospel, immediately after Jesus says, "There are some standing here who will not taste death until they see the kingdom of God has come with power" (9:1), the story of the Transfiguration is told.

Without denying the hope it holds out for the return of Christ, the *parousia*, it does seem to me that the world of the gospels is present-oriented. That, I would suggest, is both because Jesus' own people were present rather than future oriented and because a present orientation reflects the deeply Biblical truth that God IS. God reveals the Divine Name to Moses as "I AM WHO I AM" (Exodus 3:14). While God has existed and will exist, God is available to us in the present tense, sustaining all that is by that Being. While Jesus Christ may be "the same yesterday and today and forever" (Hebrews 13:8), He is also, by His own promise, "with [us] always" (Mt. 28:20). In the gospels, the locus of God's saving activity in Jesus is today. He shows forth what "Emmanuel" means: God with us, here and now.

And this brings me to the point of asking the big theological question for this whole study: so what? What is the point of slowing down, of making Sabbath time? The point is to learn to live in the present, for it is by attentiveness in the present moment that we encounter God. With regard to time, as with so many things, we Christians must become distinctly counter-cultural; we must shift from being future-oriented people to being present-oriented people. I am not arguing that we set aside the Christian hope of heaven, nor that we set aside our responsibilities or our work. I am asking that we become present to them, to find joy in them rather than seeing them primarily as a means to an end. My thinking along these lines is, I think, consistent with the gospels, but it is also, I know, highly influenced by Buddhism.

The Buddhist tradition teaches that "enlightenment" (which is, more or less, its equivalent of the Christian term "salvation") is available in the present moment. Emancipation from "unsatisfactoriness," from suffering and partiality is possible now. In *Zen and the Birds of Appetite,* Thomas Merton described "the ordinary everyday human existence" as "material for radical transformation of consciousness."[3] The ordinary events of day-to-day living are the "stuff" of our spiritual enlightenment. We must slow down in order to recognize it. Buddhism teaches me that Now is the tense and Here is the locus of God's saving activity. "Enlightenment" or "salvation" is available in each moment. One who receives it, in the words of Walpola Rahula, "lives fully in the present. Therefore he (sic) appreciates and enjoys things in the purest sense without self-projections. He is joyful, exultant, enjoying the pure life, his faculties pleased, free from anxiety, serene and peaceful."[4] This sounds remarkably like a person who manifests what, in the Galatian letter, Paul calls the "fruits of the spirit." (See Galatians 5:22-23.)

The present circumstances of our lives are crucial because it is in and through them we encounter God. Gunther Bornkamm puts it this way, "The future of God is salvation to the [one] who apprehends the present as God's present, and as the hour of salvation . . . . God's future is God's call to the present. . . ."[5] "God's future is God's call to the present"—this moment, now, is God's time and place. This is what *incarnation* means. We allow time to flow through our fingers like so much sand and, all the while, it is God timelessly present with us. Certainly this is the ultimate "wasting time"! The apostle Paul was not writing about time when he wrote, "You know what time it is, how it is now the moment for you to wake from sleep. For salvation is nearer to us now than when we became believers" (Rom. 13:11). His words reveal the essence of our relationship to time as well.[6]

And that is why I have urged throughout these pages that we must somehow take or make or accept Sabbath time, because Sabbath gives us the *gift* of time to live more fully in the present and thus to reconnect with God. We must, occasionally, stop doing in order to be. In this way we become present to the God Who IS. The Welsh poet R.S. Thomas (who is not as well known in

America as he deserves to be) makes the point with beautiful concreteness in his poem, "The Bright Field:"

> I have seen the sun break through
> to illuminate a small field
> for a while, and gone my way
> and forgotten it. But that was the pearl
> of great price, the one field that had
> the treasure in it. I realize now
> that I must give all that I have
> to possess it. Life is not hurrying
>
> on to a receding future, nor hankering after
> an imagined past. It is the turning
> aside like Moses to the miracle
> of the lit bush, to a brightness
> that seemed as transitory as your youth
> once, but is the eternity that awaits you.[7]

Thomas's poem articulates a deeply biblical spirituality of time when it tells us that "Life is not hurrying / on to a receding future, nor hankering after / an imagined past. It is the turning / aside to the miracle / . . . the eternity that awaits you." For far too many of us life is "hurrying on" and "hankering after" rather than "being present to" and "rejoicing in." One of the reasons the "lilies of the field" passage in Matthew 6:25-34 (Luke 12:22-31) appeals to us so deeply is that, again, it returns us to the realities of life.

Most of us must learn to "turn aside" in order to accept and appreciate the miracle of the present. This, after

all, is the pattern set by Jesus' own life, a pattern of engagement and withdrawal. In the central section of
Matthew's gospel Jesus is shown in confrontation with
his accusers, engaged in works of compassion, and withdrawing for prayer. At 12:15, 14:13, and 15:21, His activity is described with some form of the verb *anachoreo*
which, as I noted earlier, is usually translated "withdraw"
but means not only "go away" but also "come back." The
verb is formed from the preposition *ana* which means
"each" or "each one" and the verb *choreo* "to make room
for, to hold, to contain." Jesus withdraws precisely in
order to make room for each person and situation He
will face. Paradoxically, Jesus withdraws to be present.
And this is what we must learn to do.

Sabbath time is intended to provide moments of
"turning aside" of "withdrawal" in order to experience
our own "I am" and the great "I AM" which is God with
us. "Reflected into time, God's now unfolds for us as
past, present, and future," writes Brother David Steindl-
Rast in *Gratefulness: The Heart of Prayer*, but "it makes
no sense to speak of past and future with regard to God.
God lives in 'the now that does not pass away.'"[8] This is,
of course, the heart of the matter of a biblical spirituality
of time. It all boils down to living in the "now that does
not pass away." Our experience of that aspect of God's
time often comes to us in prayer, time for which is a fundamental element of Sabbath (though not necessarily for
"saying prayers," as I hope these reflections have made
clear).

A proper spirituality of time is one that seeks to bring life and prayer together—indeed finally to conflate them. It realizes in the arresting phrase of Simone Weil that "absolute attention is prayer." We make Sabbath in order to be attentive to what and Who is around us all the time. Reflecting on Weil's insight, the poet May Sarton wrote, "If one looks long enough at almost anything, looks with absolute attention . . . something like revelation takes place. Something is 'given,' and perhaps that something is always a reality *outside* the self."[9] That "reality outside the self" which is waiting to reveal itself is what I would call "God." God waits in time to give the Divine Self to us timelessly, to help us experience "the now that does not pass away."

It is my deep conviction that once we have had a few "peak experiences" of this sort, had experiences of "God's now," our lives will be radically transformed. When we experience human time as opening into Divine time, the character of human time changes. It becomes the matrix of delight, what Merton called the sphere of our spontaneity, "a sacramental gift in which [we] can allow [our] freedom to deploy itself in joy."[10] When we experience that time, like everything else in life, is a gift given by God, when we gratefully accept it, then we really begin to live as if, in the words of that corny and much-beloved Christmas movie, "It's a wonderful life."

In her book *A Seven Day Journey with Thomas Merton,* Esther de Waal quotes from one of the talks Merton gave in California in 1968 before he made what was to be his last journey, a pilgrimage to Asia. Merton reflected that

> If we really want prayer, we'll have to give it time. We must slow down to a human tempo and we'll begin to have time to listen. . . . But for this we have to experience time in a new way. . . . The reason why we don't take time is a feeling that we have to keep moving. This is a real sickness. Today time is a commodity, and for each one of us time is mortgaged. . . . we must approach the whole idea of time in a new way. We live in the fullness of time. Every moment is God's own good time, His *kairos*. The whole things boils down to giving ourselves in prayer a chance to realize that we have what we seek. We don't have to rush after it. It is there all the time, and if we give it time it will make itself known to us.[11]

We need to "slow down to a human tempo" and experience time as it was meant to be experienced. We already live in the "fullness of time," and we must give ourselves "a chance to realize that we have what we seek." Our hearts and flesh cry out for the living God, Who IS here, right now, among us if we but receive that Divine Presence. The call to "take time to be holy" is a call to integrate prayer and life, for they are, in fact, one. The call is to live as if all time were Sabbath time.

So, I rejoice to announce to you, it is.

Notes

Introduction

1. Henri Nouwen, *Sabbatical Journey* (New York: The Crossroad Publishing Company, 1998),.215.

2. See, for example, Stephen Hawking's *A Brief History of Time*, or Huw Price, *Time's Arrow and Archemides' Point: New Directions for the Physics of Time*, or Hans Reichenbach, *The Direction of Time*.

3. John O'Donohue, *Anam Cara: A Book of Celtic Wisdom* (New York: HarperCollins, 1997), 151.

4. Jim Forest, *Praying with Icons* (Maryknoll, New York: Orbis Books, 1997), 45.

5. Forest, *Praying with Icons*, 35.

6. David Steindl-Rast, O.S.B., *The Music of Silence* (San Francisco: HarperSanFrancisco, 1995), 5.

Chapter One: The Gift of Time

1. Bruce Anderson, "Losing Time," *Attache,* March, 1998, 67-69.

2. John Marsh, *The Fullness of Time* (London: Nisbet & Co., 1952), 1.

3. Karl Barth, *Church Dogmatics* I, 2, 14 (Edinburgh: Clark, 1956), 50.

4. Frederick Buechner, *The Sacred Journey* (San Francisco: Harper, 1982), 9-10.

5. Buechner, *The Sacred Journey*,10-11.

6. Bruce Malina, "Christ and Time: Swiss or Mediterranean?" *CBQ* 51/1 (1989), 1-31, especially pp. 11-14 on "experienced time."

7. Steindl-Rast, *The Music of Silence*, 12.

8. Philip Booth, "Original Sequence," in *King Solomon's Gardens,* Laurance Wieder, ed. (New York: Harry N. Abrams, Inc., 1994), 24-25.

9. E. Jenni, "Time," in *Interpreter's Dictionary of the Bible* George Buttrick, ed. (Nashville; Abingdon, 1962/85), 4:643.

Chapter Two: A History of Time

1. John Marsh, *The Fullness of Time*,20, 25.

2. P. C. Berg, "Time (In the Bible)," *New Catholic Encyclopedia* (New York: McGraw-Hill, 1976), 14:163.

3. Malina, "Christ and Time,"9-10.

4. Most of the material in this paragraph is from J. M. Quinn's entry on time in the *New Catholic Encyclopedia* (New York: McGraw-Hill, 1976), 4:155-160.

5. Paul Tillich, *The Protestant Era* (Chicago: University of Chicago Press, 1957), 27 and 45.

6. Oscar Cullmann, *Christ and Time* (Philadelphia: Westminster, 1950), 43.

7. Thomas Merton, *Learning to Love* (San Francisco: Harper San Francisco, 1997), 353.

Chapter Three: Time Participles

1. Tillich, *The Protestant Era*, 33. Please note that although my own preference is for inclusive language, I have maintained

the language of the author in all quotations for the sake of accuracy.

2. Thomas Merton, *Learning to Love*, 353.

3. Philip Sheldrake, *Befriending Our Desires* (Notre Dame: Ave Maria Press, 1994), 12.

4. Sheldrake, *Befriending Our Desires,* 25.

5. Benedicta Ward, *The Desert Christian* (New York: Macmillan, 1975), 178.

6. Thomas Merton, *Wisdom of the Desert* (New York: New Directions, 1960), 26.

Chapter Four: A Theology of Time

1. Thomas Merton, *Seasons of Celebration* (New York: Farrar, Straus & Giroux, 1965), 46.

2. Abraham J. Heschel, *The Sabbath* (New York: Farrar, Straus & Giroux, 1996), 6.

3. Paul Tillich, *The Eternal Now* (New York: Charles Scribners Sons, 1963), 123.

4. Hans Reichenbach, *The Direction of Time* (Berkeley: University of California Press, 1991), 8.

5. *Macbeth* V.5.19-28. In W. J. Craig (ed.), *The Complete Works of Shakespeare* (London: Oxford University Press, 1942), 1003.

6. Quoted from Helen Gardner, *The Metaphysical Poets* (Baltimore: Penguin Books, 1975), 250-251. Italics in original.

7. O'Donohue, *Anam Cara*, 174-175.

8. My thanks to The Rev. Jessica Lawrence.

9. Tillich, *The Eternal Now*, 131.

10. Evelyn Underhill, *The Spiritual Life* (New York: Harper & Bros., n.d.), 24.

11. Abraham Maslow, *Religions, Values and Peak Experiences* (Columbus: Ohio State University Press, 1964), 64.

12. Maslow, *Religions, Values and Peak Experiences*, 68.

13. Marsh, *The Fullness of Time*, 22, 24.

14. Cullmann, *Christ and Time*, 50.

15. Barth, *Church Dogmatics*, 50, 58.

16. Reichenbach, *The Direction of Time*, 3.

17. Reichenbach, *The Direction of Time*, 4.

18. Merton, *Seasons of Celebration*, 48.

19. Tillich, *The Protestant Era*, 47.

Chapter Five: The Rhythms of Time

1. Robert Cooke, interview with Owen Gingerich, "Easy Fix for Millennial Confusion," in *Newsday*. April 6, 1999, p. C8.

2. Dorothy C. Bass, "Keeping Sabbath: Reviving a Christian Practice," *Christian Century* 114/1 (January 1-8, 1997), 12.

3. Malina, "Christ and Times," 3.

4. Jacob Milgrom, "Jubilee: A Rallying Cry for Today's Oppressed," *Bible Review* 13/2 (1997), 16, 48. And see also Wilred Harrington, o.p., "Jubilee: Challenge to Monopoly," *Spirituality* 4/18 (1998), 176-178.

5. To those who are interested, I commend two editions of the Rule: Timothy Fry, O.S.B., *The Rule of St. Benedict* (Collegeville, Mn.: The Liturgical Press, 1981) and Anthony Meisel and M. L. delMastro, *The Rule of St. Benedict* (Garden City, N.Y.: Doubleday, 1975). Esther de Waal's *Seeking God*: The Way of St. Benedict (Collegeville, Minn.: The Liturgical Press, 1984) is a wonderful reflection on the rule in the "everyday" life of non-monastics.

6. Kathleen Norris, *The Cloister Walk* (New York: Riverhead Books, 1996), xiii.

7. Steindl-Rast, *The Music of Silence*, 121-122.

8. Forest, *Praying with Icons*, 49.

9. Merton, *Seasons of Celebration*, 52.

10. Norris, *The Cloister Walk,* xiii.

11. Bass, "Keeping Sabbath," 13.

12. Bill Wylie Kellerman, "Re-Creation of the Sabbath: An Interview with Arthur Waskow," *Call to Action* (June, 1997), 6.

13. Bass, "Keeping Sabbath," 12.

14. J. Morgenstern, "Sabbath," in *Interpreter's Dictionary of the Bible*, George Buttrick, ed. (Nashville: Abingdon, 1962/85), 4:135.

15. Morgenstern, "Sabbath," 139-140.

16. Morgenstern, "Sabbath,"135.

17. Forest, *Praying with Icons*, 85-86.

18. Tilden Edwards, *Sabbath Time* (Nashville: Upper Room, 1992), 18.

19. Heschel, *The Sabbath*, 13.

20. Heschel, *The Sabbath*, 15.

21. Heschel, *The Sabbath*, 3.

22. Edwards, *Sabbath Time,* 39.

Chapter Six: "A Sabbath Rest for the People of God"

1. *The Book of Common Prayer* (New York: Oxford University Press, 1979), 99.

2. Joan Chittister, "Recovering Lost Sabbath," reprinted in *Call to Action* (June, 1997), 2.

3. Thomas Merton, *New Seeds of Contemplation* (New York: New Directions, 1972), 35.

4. Merton, *New Seeds of Contemplation,* 35.

5. Edwards, *Sabbath Time,* 29.

6. Heschel, *The Sabbath*, 6.

7. Heschel, *The Sabbath*, 28.

8. Heschel, *The Sabbath*, 73-74.

9. Heschel, *The Sabbath*, 30.

10. Forest, *Praying with Icons*, 38.

11. Hans Reichenbach, *The Direction of Time,* 1.

12. Berg, "Time (In the Bible)," 14:163.

13. S. A. Cunningham, "Time (In Theology)," *New Catholic Encyclopedia* (New York: McGraw Hill, 1976), 14: 164.

14. Catherine Aslanoff, (ed.) and Paul Meyendorff (trans.), *The Incarnate God* (New York: St. Vladimir's Seminary Press, 1995), II: 198.

15. Most of this discussion is taken from my article "Praying for the Living and the Dead: Remembering," in *Rethinking the Spiritual Works of Mercy*, F. A. Eigo, ed. (Philadelphia: Villanova University Press, 1993), 164.

16. T. S. Eliot, *Four Quartets* (New York: Harcourt, Brace, Jovanovich, 1971), 59.

17. Bass, "Keeping Sabbath," 12.

18. Chittister, "Recovering Lost Sabbath," 2.

19. O'Donohue, *Anam Cara*, 129.

20. Heschel, *The Sabbath*, 14.

21. Bass, "Keeping Sabbath," 15.

22. Edwards, *Sabbath Time*, 62.

23. O'Donohue, *Anam Cara*, 152.

24. Esther de Waal, *The Celtic Way of Prayer* (London: Hodder & Stoughton, 1996), 177.

25. David Steindl-Rast, O.S.B., *Gratefulness: The Heart of Prayer* (New York: Paulist Press, 1984), 204, 12.

26. Edwards, *Sabbath Time*, 70-71.

Chapter Seven: No Time Like the Present

1. O'Donohue, *Anam Cara*, 191.

2. Malina, "Christ and Time," 4.

3. Thomas Merton, *Zen and the Birds of Appetite* (New York: New Directions, 1968), 51.

4. Walpola Rahula, *What the Buddha Taught* (New York: Grove Press, 1974), 43. The exclusive language is that of the original.

5. Gunther Bornkamm, *Jesus of Nazareth* (London: Hodder and Stoughton, 1960), 93.

6. For a slightly expanded version of my ideas on the Buddhist-Christian connection here, see my article, "Amazing, Ordinary Rapture," in *Living Prayer* 21/1 (1988), 16-17.

7. R. S. Thomas, *Poems of R. S. Thomas* (Fayetteville: University of Arkansas Press, 1985), 104-105.

8. Steindl-Rast, *Gratefulness: The Heart of Prayer*, 133.

9. May Sarton, *Journal of a Solitude* (New York: W. W. Norton, 1973), 99.

10. Thomas Merton, *Seasons of Celebration*, 46.

11. Thomas Merton, quoted in Esther de Waal, *A Seven Day Journey with Thomas Merton* (Guilford, Surrey: Eagle, 1992), 43.

Bibliography

Anderson, Bruce. "Losing Time," *Attache* (March, 1998) 66–69.

Aslanoff, Catherine (ed.) and Paul Meyendorff (transl.), *The Incarnate God* (New York: St. Vladimir's Seminary Press, 1995).

Barth, Karl. *Church Dogmatics* (Vol. I.2) (Edinburgh: T & T Clark, 1956).

Bass, Dorothy C., "Keeping Sabbath: Reviving a Christian Practice," *The Christian Century* 114/1 (Jan. 1–8, 1997) 12–16.

Berg, P.C., "Time (In the Bible)," *New Catholic Encyclopedia* (New York: McGraw Hill, 1976).

Bornkamm, Gunther. *Jesus of Nazareth* (London: Hodder & Stoughton, 1960).

Buechner, Frederick, *The Sacred Journey* (San Francisco: Harper, 1982).

Chittister, Joan, "Recovering the Lost Sabbath," *Call to Action,* (June, 1997), 1–2.

Cullmann, Oscar. *Christ and Time* (Philadelphia: Westminster, 1950).

Cunningham, S.A., "Time (In Theology)," *New Catholic Encyclopedia* (New York: McGraw Hill, 1976).

deWaal, Esther. *The Celtic Way of Prayer* (London: Hodder & Stoughton, 1996).

————. *Seeking God: The Way of St. Benedict* (Collegeville, Mn.: The Liturgical Press, 1984).

————. *A Seven Day Journey with Thomas Merton* (Guilford, Surrey: Eagle, 1992).

Edwards, Tilden. *Sabbath Time* (Nashville: Upper Room, 1992).

Eliot, T.S. *Four Quartets* (New York: Harcourt, Brace, Jovanovich, 1971).

Forest, Jim. *Praying with Icons* (Maryknoll, New York: Orbis Books, 1997).

Fry, Timothy, O.S.B. (ed.), *The Rule of St. Benedict* (Collegeville, Mn.: The Liturgical Press, 1981).

Glatt, D.S., "Sabbath," *Harper's Bible Dictionary.*

Harrington, Wilfred. "Jubilee: Challenge to Monopoly," *Spirituality* 4/18 (1998) 176–178.

Hawking, Stephen. *A Brief History of Time* (New York: Bantam Books, 1988).

Heschel, Abraham J. *The Sabbath* (New York: Farrar, Straus, Giroux, 1996).

Hochschild, Arlie. *The Time Bind* (New York: Metropolitan Books, 1997).

Jenni, E., "Time," *Interpreter's Dictionary of the Bible* (Nashville: Abingdon, 1962/85).

Malina, Bruce. "Christ and Time: Swiss or Mediterranean?" *Catholic Biblical Quarterly* 51/1 (1998) 1–31.

Marsh, John. *The Fullness of Time* (London: Nisbet & Co., 1952).

Maslow, Abraham H. *Religions, Values and Peak Experiences* (Columbus: Ohio State University Press, 1964).

Meisel, Anthony & del Mastro, M. (eds.). *The Rule of St. Benedict* (New York: Image, 1975).

Merton, Thomas. *Learning to Love, Christine Bochen, editor* (San Francisco: Harper, 1997).

————. *New Seeds of Contemplation* (New York: New Directions, 1972).

————. *Seasons of Celebration* (New York: Farrar, Straus, Giroux, 1965).

————. *The Wisdom of the Desert* (New York: New Directions, 1960).

————. *Zen and the Birds of Appetite* (New York: New Directions, 1968).

Milgrom, Jacob. "Jubilee: A Rallying Cry for Today's Oppressed," *Bible Review* 13/2 (1997) 16, 48.

Morgenstern, J. "Sabbath," *Interpreter's Dictionary of the Bible* (Nashville: Abingdon, 1962/85).

Norris, Kathleen. *The Cloister Walk* (New York: Riverhead Books, 1996).

O'Donohue, John. *Anam Cara: A Book of Celtic Wisdom* (New York: HarperCollins, 1997).

Quinn, J.M. "Time," *New Catholic Encyclopedia* (New York: McGraw Hill, 1976).

Rahula, Walpola. *What the Buddha Taught* (New York: Grove Press, 1974).

Reichenbach, Hans. *The Direction of Time* (Berkeley: University of California Press, 1991).

Sarton, May. *Journal of a Solitude* (New York: W.W.Norton, 1973).

Sheldrake, Philip, *Befriending Our Desires* (Notre Dame: Ave Maria Press, 1994).

Steindl-Rast, David. O.S.B. *Gratefulness: The Heart of Prayer* (New York: Paulist Press, 1984).

————. *The Music of Silence* (San Francisco: Harprer, 1995).

Thomas, R.S. *Poems of R.S.Thomas* (Fayetteville: University of Arkansas Press, 1985).

Thurston, Bonnie. "Amazing, Ordinary Rapture," *Living Prayer* 21/2 (1988) 16–17.

———. "Praying for the Living and the Dead: Remembering," in *Rethinking the Spiritual Works of Mercy,* F.A. Eigo (ed.) (Philadelphia: Villanova University Press, 1993).

Tillich, Paul. *The Protestant Era* (Chicago: University of Chicago Press, 1957).

———. *The Eternal Now* (New York: Charles Scribners Sons, 1963).

Underhill, Evelyn. *The Spiritual Life* (New York: Harper & Bros., n.d.).

Ward, Benedicta. *The Desert Christian* (New York: Macmillan, 1975).

Whiteman, Michael. *Philosophy of Space and Time* (New York: Humanities Press, 1967).

Wylie-Kellerman, Bill. "Re-Creation of Sabbath: an Interview with Arthur Waskow," *Call to Action* (June, 1997), 3–6.